# THE SOVIET UNION AND ARMS CONTROL:

# A SUPERPOWER DILEMMA

# THE SOVIET UNION
# AND
# ARMS CONTROL:
# A SUPERPOWER DILEMMA

*by*

Roman Kolkowicz
Matthew P. Gallagher
Benjamin S. Lambeth

*with*

Walter C. Clemens, Jr.
Peter W. Colm

THE JOHNS HOPKINS PRESS
Baltimore and London

The Johns Hopkins Press, Baltimore, Maryland 21218
The Johns Hopkins Press Ltd., London

Library of Congress Catalog Card Number 77-128009

ISBN 0-8018-1185-6 (clothbound edition)
ISBN 0-8018-1186-4 (paperback edition)

# Contents

## CONTENTS

# Preface

THIS STUDY WAS PREPARED in the International and Social Studies Division of the Institute for Defense Analyses and is based on a research report commissioned by the United States Arms Control and Disarmament Agency. Its basic purpose was to analyze the perceptions, motivations, incentives, and constraints that shape Soviet policies on arms control. Based on extensive research, including examination of Soviet sources, the book focuses on the political and strategic factors in Soviet arms control policies.

Though the study is the joint product of the Arms Control Project members, the several parts of the study were prepared by the individual members: the Introduction and "The Arms Control Issue in the Soviet Political Context" (chapter 1) by Matthew P. Gallagher; "Soviet-American Strategic Relations: Implications for Arms Control" (chapter 2) and "Conclusions and Projections" (chapter 6) by Roman Kolkowicz, who was also the project leader; "Nuclear Proliferation and Soviet Arms Control Policy" (chapter 3) by Benjamin S. Lambeth; "Sino-Soviet Relations and the China Factor in Soviet Arms Control Policies" (chapter 4) by Peter Colm; and "Soviet Policies Toward Europe: Implications for Arms Control" (chapter 5) by Walter C. Clemens, Jr. The views and opinions expressed in this paper are entirely those of the authors and do not imply the endorsement of the Arms Control and Disarmament Agency or other agencies of the United States government.

The members of the project benefited in various ways from the generous assistance of Dr. Chester L. Cooper, director of the International and Social Studies Division; Mr. Walter Hahn and Mr. Joseph Yager, deputy directors of the Division; and Dr. Harland B. Moulton and Mr. Michael Durkee of the Arms Control and Disarmament Agency. Mrs. Jean Shirhall edited the manuscript, and Miss Rosemary Hayes assisted in the research. Special recognition is due Mrs. Thelma Davis, who typed the several drafts of the study.

R. K.
May 1970

# Introduction

THE STRATEGIC ARMS LIMITATION talks which opened in Helsinki on November 17, 1969, mark the beginning of a new era in Soviet-American strategic relations. For a decade or more, the two nuclear powers have geared their strategic policies to the dynamics of an expanding missile technology. Each has sought to outdo the other, not so much because the results could be translated into practical political uses, but because it was felt that a failure to keep pace might forfeit some future advantage to the adversary. Almost without intending it, the two powers have derived a security of sorts from this effort—a security based on a tacit understanding that neither could destroy the other without suffering destruction in return.

Now, for the first time, the two nuclear powers have begun an effort to reinforce this tacit understanding with explicit agreements concerning the nature and numbers of weapon systems that each will deploy. If their effort succeeds, the urgency of their strategic competition will be relaxed, and a quieter atmosphere will be created for dealing with the political problems that divide them. If they fail, a new round of strategic competition can be expected, with all the uncertainties that this will bring in its train. Whatever the outcome, it can be predicted with assurance that the mechanisms of international security that have operated thus far in the nuclear age are in for some extensive overhauls in the 1970s.

What has brought the United States to accept the need for a retooling of international security mechanisms has been set forth in abundant detail in presidential statements, public discussion, and technical literature. The key factor, these data make clear, is the emergence of new technology which affects the on-target effectiveness of nuclear-missile weapons. MIRVs, ABMs, and improvements in warhead accuracy are among the innovations made possible by this new technology. The possession of this new technology by both superpowers, the American analyses assert, would work to undermine the tacit understanding on which the present deterrence relationship rests. The American rationale for entering the strategic arms limitation talks, therefore, is pragmatic and prudential. It is aimed at preventing a headlong rush into a new technological competition, the outcome of which could well be a degradation of the precarious security which the present situation provides.

The Soviet rationale is less easy to define, largely because there is no public discussion in the Soviet Union of sensitive foreign policy issues. It can be assumed that the Soviet Union is affected by much the same considerations that govern the American approach to the issue. Indeed, Foreign Minister Gromyko made these concerns explicit in his speech to the Supreme Soviet in June 1968, in which he first announced the Soviet Union's acceptance of the idea of beginning the talks. Referring to the new risks and uncertainties which a new round of Soviet-American arms competition would create, he reflected: "There are problems which are sometimes blunted by time. But there are also problems which accumulate new complications and dangers with the passing of time. Thus, life raises the problem of discontinuing the arms race, the problem of disarmament."

It is not enough, however, to leave the question of Soviet attitudes and objectives at this general level of common sense assumptions. Today the two nuclear powers stand at a crossroads where important new strategic decisions are required and where each has the opportunity to make significant policy departures which may vitally affect the course of international security in the 1970s. How the two powers respond to this challenge will hinge critically on how each perceives the intentions of the other. Just as the Soviet Union's willingness to consider strategic arms limitation agreements will be determined in considerable measure by its assessments of the United States as a willing and receptive negotiatory partner, so will American strategies and arms control policies in the coming years necessarily have to consider Soviet strategic motives and objectives.

The purpose of this book is to shed as much light as possible on these questions by systematically examining the various considerations bearing on Moscow's approach to the strategic arms limitation issue. The book is divided into six chapters.

Chapter 1 provides a basic framework for the study by attempting to view the issue as the Soviet leaders themselves would view it. It examines the more "subjective" factors which work to determine Moscow's attitude toward the talks—the internal political dynamics of the Soviet decision-making process. It places the issue in the context of the wide range of policies and political concerns that bear on the leadership's decisions. It examines the political factions, institutions, and functional groupings in the Soviet system that may be regarded as favorably disposed toward the talks, and which most likely have been influential in shaping the regime's present posture on the issue. It examines, also, the groups whose nature, political biases, or institutional interests would incline them to oppose strategic arms limitation agreements and East-West détente. This chapter also considers such factors as the stability of the current Soviet collective leadership arrangement, the ability of the Brezhnev-Kosygin regime to cope with the complex problems sure to be raised by the strategic arms limitation talks, and the sensitivity of Soviet policy to fluctuations both in the political attitudes, interests, and alignments in the Soviet leadership structure, and in the course of the negotiations themselves.

Chapter 2 considers the broad strategic context in which Soviet attitudes toward the strategic arms limitation issue have evolved. It focuses on the Soviet-American strategic relationship, its historical evolution, its present characteristics, and likely future developments which will bear upon the security needs and perceptions of the Soviet Union. It examines such questions as (1) Soviet perceptions of the adversary; (2) Soviet assessments of the changing political utility of strategic nuclear forces; (3) current Soviet attitudes toward the prevailing strategic balance in terms of its stability and Soviet security; and (4) the interdependencies between the Soviet-American strategic relationship—both present and projected—and Moscow's apparent desire to explore the possibility of a strategic arms limitation agreement. It addresses not only the specific strategic motivations governing the current Soviet interest in arms limitations, but also the closely related questions of changing Soviet views on the role of force in international politics and on the evolving nature of nuclear-age superpower relations.

Chapters 3, 4, and 5 examine, respectively, three of the more critical "external" variables which will affect the Soviet Union's security perceptions and arms control interests in the coming years: (1) the problem of nuclear proliferation—its prospects and likely consequences for Soviet policy and international stability; (2) the evolving Sino-Soviet relationship and possible developments that might bear on Moscow's arms control dispositions; and (3) the European factor, particularly Soviet interests in West Germany and in the bloc countries of Eastern Europe, and the likely relevance of alternative developments in these areas to the Soviet-American arms control prospects.

The Conclusions attempt to tie up the study by offering some practical judgments concerning the Soviet Union's negotiatory stance in the strategic arms limitation talks. Drawing on the evidence and analyses presented in the preceding chapters, it attempts to project: (1) possible Soviet objectives in the talks; (2) the criteria which the Soviet Union would be likely to apply in assessing the negotiability of any particular arms limitation scheme; (3) various possible alternative outcomes in the talks, and the critical factors and circumstances which might affect their prospects for success; and (4) the implications of Moscow's policy for future U.S. strategy, foreign policy, and diplomacy.

# THE SOVIET UNION AND ARMS CONTROL:

# A SUPERPOWER DILEMMA

# 1

## The SALT Issue in the Soviet Political Context

IT WOULD BE RELATIVELY easy to predict Soviet policy in the strategic arms limitation talks (SALT) if the only factors to be considered were the military costs and benefits of the various arms control schemes. Other factors, however, will affect the judgments and actions of the Soviet policy-makers who will decide the issue. Their responses to challenges and opportunities are not automatic; they see the world darkly, like the rest of men, through the glass of their own preconceptions and limitations of experience. Their judgments are affected by other interests and commitments and by the pressures of their office. It would be surprising if Soviet policy were a mirror reflection of the country's needs and opportunities, or if it meshed perfectly with all the contours of the strategic situation as seen from Washington. Soviet policy, in other words, is a product of invention as well as need.

This chapter is devoted to a discussion of these political factors. It is divided into three parts. The

1

first examines the strategic arms limitation issue as it presents itself to the policy-makers, in the context of a wide range of policies and political concerns. The second examines the pressures that may be brought to bear on their deliberations by the groups and institutions in Soviet society that may be affected by the decisions. The third assesses the considerations relevant to the political character of the Soviet leadership which may affect the substance and continuity of Soviet policy on the issue.

## THE ISSUE AND ITS RAMIFICATIONS

Soviet policy-makers have probably faced few issues in recent years that have been more complex than the arms control question. It concerns more than military security alone; it concerns the whole range of policies and programs based on the present structure of Soviet-American relations. At the heart of the issue is a complex military-political question: Should the Soviet Union maintain the pace of its military competition with the United States, or should it relax this effort, seeking by diplomatic means to bring about a corresponding slowdown in the United States?

In weighing the alternatives, the Soviet policy-makers would be concerned, first of all, with the strategic considerations which would be likely to suggest strong arguments in favor of scaling down the arms race. The military balance between the Soviet Union and the United States may now be optimal from the standpoint of the Soviet Union's security interests and great-power status. Over the past few years, the Soviet Union has acquired a credible retaliatory capability through the rapid expansion of its land-based intercontinental ballistic missile forces (ICBMs), and through the dispersal and hardening of launching sites. In numbers of launchers, at least, these forces are now equal, if not superior, to the comparable American forces. A tapering off of the arms race at the present time would serve to fix the relationship at a point that would ensure equality to the Soviet Union in this critical dimension of military power.[1]

A continuation of the arms race might put the Soviet Union in a progressively worse position. The next few years in weapons developments will place heavy demands on highly advanced scientific and technological capabilities—resources in which the United States seems more generously endowed than the Soviet Union. The nature of future arms competition is suggested by weapons developments already programmed on both sides: MIRVs (multiple independently targeted reentry vehicles) to overwhelm ABM (antiballistic missile) defenses; and FOBSs (fractional orbital bombardment system) to evade early warning. The dynamics of the interaction process can be expected to produce even more exotic refinements on these various countering and offsetting devices, which would undermine the

---

[1] According to official American data, the relationship between American and Soviet strategic offensive missile launchers at the end of 1970 is:

|       | U.S.  | U.S.S.R. |
|-------|-------|----------|
| ICBMs | 1,054 | 1,290    |
| SLBMs | 656   | 30       |

See a report to the Congress by Richard Nixon, President of the United States, *U.S. Foreign Policy for the 1970s; A New Strategy for Peace*, February 18, 1970, p. 120.

mutual confidence on which the deterrence relationship has come to rest. Therefore, the question for the Soviet Union is not merely whether the present military balance is satisfactory, but whether it is more satisfactory than a situation resulting from a continuation of the arms race.

Much the same considerations apply to the other major element of the strategic equation, the ABMs. The Soviet Union has been developing an ABM system in the Moscow defense zone since the early 1960s. In many ways, it has been conducting a race against time, since changing operational requirements and improvements in technology have generated increasing pressures for adjustments in design and equipment. This whole investment of time and national energies is now threatened by the development of MIRV capabilities in the United States. The Moscow ABM system will retain some value by complicating American targeting problems and as a prestige symbol, but its ability to defend the Moscow area stands to be reduced sharply. A natural reaction in this situation—particularly for those closely associated with the system—would be to urge a redoubling of efforts to redeem the investment already made. Another reaction, however, and one more closely attuned to the realities of the situation, would be to regard further efforts as throwing good money after bad.

Proponents of the latter argument would have good ground for saying that an arms control agreement affecting defensive missile systems would not hurt, and might help, the Soviet Union as far as its over-all defense posture was concerned. Stopping or limiting the U.S. ABM program would have some value for the

4

Soviet Union. From the strategic point of view, any increment to the defense degrades the relative effectiveness of the offensive forces in question. Whether those outside the military academies and the general staff would be much impressed by the subtleties involved in such calculations may be open to question. But no particular subtlety is needed to recognize that the deployment of ABMs in the United States works to generate pressures in the Soviet Union for countermeasures.

Economic considerations also provide arguments for the limitation of the strategic weapons competition. The economic burdens of the arms race have long worked to constrain the Soviet Union's ability to satisfy consumer needs and to make the investments in new plant and machinery necessary to ensure future economic growth. Military expenditures have increased annually since 1965, and, relative to the growth of the economy as a whole, investments have declined during this same period. The military drain on the economy has affected precisely those high-quality resources, human and material, needed for economic modernization.

Despite the efforts by the Brezhnev-Kosygin regime to correct some of the economic problems, there has been only a partial recovery from the declining performance trends that emerged in the early 1960s. The trend in the growth rate of the GNP has tended to flatten out, and the capital-output ratio—that is, the ability of the economy to translate additional resources into additional output—has been worsening. The sharp rise in defense expenditures, occasioned by the expansion of the strategic forces, has forced the regime to scrimp on allocations to other economic uses, particularly investment, which might have worked to alleviate some of the problems. As a result, the regime has found it difficult to meet its growing commitments, with little prospect of relief as long as defense expenditures continue to rise at a rapid rate.[2]

This bind on resources has been a source of obvious embarrassment to the Soviet leaders, forcing them to postpone, or scale down, other programs of political importance. Politburo member Suslov admitted as much when, in a speech in Sofia on June 2, 1965, he expressed regret that defense requirements prevented the Soviet Union from doing all that it would like in improving the people's welfare.[3] Kosygin made a similar statement at the Twenty-third Party Congress: "If matters depended solely on us," he said, "we would surely have made substantial cuts in military spending."[4] Brezhnev added his voice to this litany of *mea culpa*'s in his pre-election speech in 1966. Asserting that "expenditures for the army and armaments are a great burden for the budget, for our national economy," he said that the party would like to drop "at least part of this load" from the people's shoulders, but could not take this course because the "situation" did not permit it.[5] Politburo member Polyanskii highlighted another effect of the economic bind when, in a *Kommunist* article, he complained that agriculture was being short-

[2] For a fuller discussion of these developments, see U.S., Congress, Joint Economic Committee, Subcommittee on Foreign Economic Policy, *Soviet Economic Performance: 1966–67*, 90th Congress, 2d Session (Washington, D.C.: Government Printing Office, May 1968).

[3] *Rabotnichesko Delo* (Sofia), June 4, 1965.

[4] Radio Moscow, Domestic Service, April 6, 1966.

[5] Radio Moscow, Domestic Service, April 10, 1966.

changed in investment allocations.[6] More recent commentary on official plan and budgetary data has indicated that these problems continue to exert a depressing influence on the economy.

To what extent an arms control agreement might alleviate these problems cannot be calculated precisely. But no detailed information is needed to suggest the scale of savings to be derived from an agreement that would halt the further deployment of strategic offensive and defensive missile systems. The expansion of these forces has been the main factor affecting the rise in Soviet military expenditures in the late 1960s. No doubt other military programs would be standing in the wings to claim a lion's share of the savings to be derived from a limitation of strategic forces, but in an economic system in which resources are critically scarce, even a few hundred million rubles left over would constitute a sizable prize. The prospect of deriving savings of this, or greater, magnitude would be a significant factor affecting Soviet attitudes toward arms control.

Alongside these arguments in favor of strategic arms limitation are other considerations which would incline the Soviets to take a cautious approach. In the first place, there is the natural human tendency to shrink from a radical departure from accustomed concepts and practices. Arms control is "unnatural" for a great power—particularly one whose history and ideology have created an almost mystical fixation on "defense" in the national ethos.

This tendency would be reinforced by genuine sus-

[6] *Kommunist,* vol. 14 (September 1967).

7

picions concerning American motivations in the strategic arms talks. Some policies of the Nixon administration—for example, the deployment of the Safeguard ABM system—have served to reinforce these suspicions. The Soviet propaganda charge that American policy is dominated by the military-industrial complex probably reflects a genuine concern.

Beyond this, the Soviet policy-makers would have to consider the impact of their choice on their relationships with their allies and on the whole structure of their security arrangements in Europe. Since these arrangements are justified on the ground that collective measures of defense are necessitated by the threat from the West, they have a vested interest in maintaining at least the appearance of continued East-West tensions. It is equally true, of course, that western defense arrangements are based on a similar assumption about the threat from the East, and the Soviet policy-makers no doubt recognize the mischief they could play by working to undermine that assumption. On the whole, however, they are more likely to be concerned with what an arms control agreement might mean for their own alliance interests, which would no doubt count against the advisability of seeking such an agreement.

The balance that the Soviet policy-makers might strike between domestic and international requirements would probably not be tipped sharply in one direction or the other. In a sense, the situation resembles the dilemma they faced in the spring and summer of 1968 when they were considering what course to adopt with respect to Czechoslovakia. Then, too, the international implications seemed to point in one direction and the domestic implications in another. The parallel cannot be pushed too far, but it serves at least to point up the fact that the values by which the Soviet policy-makers weigh the pros and cons of an issue do not necessarily coincide with those that might seem reasonable to an outside observer.

## THE POLITICAL FORCES IN CONTENTION

It is inevitable that there will be differences of opinion among the policy-makers and that the special-interest groups and institutions will try to affect Soviet policy as the talks proceed. To assess the effect these pressures may have, it is necessary to examine the forces in contention and the political influence they command.

On one side of the issue are the forces favoring the possibility of strategic arms limitation agreements with the United States. Most observers would probably agree that Premier Kosygin was a principal architect of the consensus that has formed among political leaders around this line. He has permitted himself to be identified as the principal spokesman for the Soviet Union on this policy, which implies his willingness to accept all the political risks that go with that identification. It is hard to say which of the other leaders and higher officials of the regime may be counted among his collaborators and followers. But it seems likely that they include the men who, like Kosygin, have invested their careers and political interests in the business of managing the national economy. They may be described as the economic rationalizers in the regime.

9

Arms control for them is a means to achieve economic gains by loosening the bind on national resources.

Below the top leaders and administrators, there are other groups well positioned in the Soviet hierarchy to affect arms control policy. Among them are the scientists and technical experts with special responsibilities in defense-related fields. It is known from numerous private contacts with these individuals over the years that many of them hold views favorable to the idea of seeking arms control agreements with the United States. While scientists, as a group, do not have an effective institutional base for developing professional opinion on general policy issues, individual scientists can acquire ad hoc importance on specific issues. Even where they lack direct access to the highest policy-making bodies, there are many formal and informal channels provided by the Soviet committee system of government which scientists can use to make their influence felt. If all else fails, there is the underground press, which many scientists, along with other intellectuals, have used in recent years to bring their views to official attention. The widely publicized statement by academician Sakharov in 1968, with its eloquent plea for bringing an end to the arms race, is only the most famous example of this form of special pleading by scientists.[7]

The influence of scientific opinion has its greatest effect, not on the broad issues of global policy, but on the technical issues involved in the evaluation of weapons systems and strategies. Needless to say, there is

[7] For many other examples, see "In Quest of Justice," *Problems of Communism*, July-August and September-October 1968 (special issues).

no public evidence that would identify the lineup of Soviet scientific opinion on a question such as the effectiveness of ABMs. But if American scientific opinion can be taken as a gauge of the world scientific community, it seems a good bet that a question such as this is at least a subject of controversy among Soviet scientists. Indeed, the inconsistencies and apparent contradictions that surface from time to time in Soviet public statements on ABMs would seem to reflect skepticism among the experts. It is hard to believe that the Soviet leadership would, as it did after 1966, substitute lame claims about an ability to shoot down "some" enemy rockets for the former boasts about the invincibility of the system if Soviet scientific opinion had remained sanguine about the system.

A third group having a special interest in the issue is the arms control professionals—the foreign policy specialists in the government and academic bureaucracies who have acquired a professional identification with the arms control issue. It is perhaps an oversimplification to describe this disparate association of officials and scholars as a special-interest group in any strict sense of the word, but the individuals exert a special force in the formulation of policy.[8] They act as the main purveyors of the ideas that serve to define the scope and substance of the regime's internal dialogue on the issue. They stand to profit in a personal and professional way by the regime's continuing interest in the subject. Their role is not conducive to bold or

[8] For an illuminating discussion of the historical role of these experts on the arms control issue, see Franklyn Griffiths, "Inner Tensions in the Soviet Approach to 'Disarmament,'" *International Journal*, vol. XXII, no. 4 (Autumn 1967).

fresh ideas, but if such ideas were to emerge in the Soviet Union, they would come from this group. They do, at least, have incentives to keep the subject active on the official agenda, and, to this extent, they are likely to favor the idea of taking initiatives on the issue.

These forces—the economic rationalizers, the scientists, and the arms control professionals—now seem to enjoy a favorable position in the internal competition for influence over the policy-makers on the strategic arms limitation issue.

On the other side of the issue are the forces opposed to the idea of linking the country's security to an arrangement of mutual accommodation with the United States. They include the ideologues of the party apparatus whose mental outlook is rooted in a suspicious, and even paranoic, view of western intentions and whose professional interests are dependent on the regime's continued adherence to this outlook in official policy. They also include members of the industrial managerial bureaucracy who have made their careers in defense production and who have acquired, as a consequence, a stake in the continuation of high-tension relations with the United States.

The most visible opposition to the regime's policy on the strategic arms limitation talks, however, is based in the military establishment. Probably all western observers would agree that an arms control agreement of the scope and character of some of the schemes likely to be considered in connection with the current talks would pose a threat to interests which military officers, as a whole, share. It is a truism, demonstrated by the history of Soviet military policy, that the fortunes of the military establishment are likely to rise or fall in accordance with the temperature fluctuations of the international climate. As one refreshingly candid military spokesman put it some years ago, the question of the possibility of war was more than a theoretical question, because on it hinged the question of the levels of military allocations.[9] There is a sense, thus, in which arms control poses a threat to the military establishment and creates an issue on which the military are likely to rally.

This is not to say that all elements of the military establishment are equally threatened, or that all are likely to resist strategic arms limitation agreements with equal vigor. The Strategic Rocket Forces (SRF) and the Air Defense Forces (PVO), which are services based on the strategic offensive and defensive missile systems, have much more at stake in the outcome of the issue than other branches of the armed forces. Both have demonstrated remarkable powers of self-defense in the bureaucratic infighting that determines budget allocations and role assignments in the country's overall defense posture. Despite changing Soviet perceptions of the relative utilities of strategic and conventional power in recent years, the SRF have succeeded in beating off all challenges to their right to be called the "main" branch of the armed forces.[10] The PVO have been equally prickly about defending their rights. They have fought a rearguard action against the SRF for a number of years to win doctrinal acceptance of

[9] Colonel I. Sidelnikov, *Krasnaia zvezda*, September 22, 1965.

[10] It is striking testimony to the SRF's success that the third edition of Sokolovskii's *Military Strategy*, issued in 1968, contains hardly a reflection of the flexible response concepts that have come into vogue in Soviet military circles.

the view that the strategic defense is a form of military action equal in importance to the strategic offense.[11] At least some of the articles inspired by this campaign appear to have been intended to serve notice on the regime that the PVO would be less than eager for an arms control agreement affecting defensive missiles.

That these military attitudes are likely to be brought forcibly to bear on the policy-makers is suggested by the continuing resistance of the military to the arms control idea over the years. The record goes back at least to 1960, when Khrushchev complained of the opposition he was meeting on the issue from his military advisers.[12] Opposition to the 1963 Test Ban Treaty was openly displayed in the military press. The tactic used was a conspiracy of silence—a military-press blackout of all commentary and favorable publicity on the Test Ban Treaty at a time when *Pravda* and other Soviet newspapers were celebrating the event with editorials and pages of congratulatory letters from abroad. The blackout even affected Malinovskii's Navy Day "Order of the Day" promulgated a few days after the treaty had been initialed. It contained no mention of the treaty, but included a strangely inappropriate reminder that the "imperialists" were working to hinder an easing of international tension.[13]

[11] For the beginning of this campaign, see the review of Sokolovskii's book in *Voyennyy vestnik*, January 1963. Other examples of more recent articles on the same theme include Colonel S. Krupnov, *Krasnaia zvezda*, January 7, 1966; and Colonel I. Zavyalov, *Krasnaia zvezda*, March 30 and 31, 1967.

[12] Remarks at a luncheon for Cyrus Eaton. See *Pravda*, September 28, 1960. It is a matter of considerable significance that *Kransnaia zvezda*, the Defense Ministry's newspaper, carried no account of these remarks.

[13] For an analysis of these events, see Victor Zorza, "Military

Military opposition to the idea of the current strategic arms limitation talks has been evident since the matter came under serious consideration in the Soviet government.[14] After Gromyko's announcement of the Soviet Union's willingness to accept the talks in June 1968, the opposition became more obvious. Military spokesmen consistently refrained from mentioning the arms control talks in speeches and articles. The military press reported incomplete accounts of government declarations on arms control, omitting statements favorable to the missile talks.[15] A few military authors

---

Critics of Mr. K," *The Manchester Guardian*, October 4, 1963.

[14] See, for example, an article by Lieutenant General I. Zavyalov that appeared in *Krasnaia zvezda* in two installments on March 30 and 31, 1967—two months after President Johnson's offer of the talks and six weeks after Kosygin's London press conference. While not addressing the talks idea directly, Zavyalov's article implied opposition to the idea of limiting ABMs by arguing strongly for the importance of "strategic defense" in the country's over-all defense posture.

[15] The first case of tampering involved Gromyko's speech to the United Nations on October 3, 1968. The speech contained several paragraphs on strategic arms limitation, including a reiteration of the Soviet Union's willingness to begin talks with the United States. The next day, as expected, the major Moscow newspapers carried faithful accounts of the speech, but *Krasnaia zvezda*, the Defense Ministry's newspaper, carried only a compressed version—one which was edited in such a way as to omit any mention of strategic arms limitation.

A second case involved the Foreign Ministry's statement urging prompt action on the arms limitation talks, which was issued on the eve of President Nixon's inauguration. The *Krasnaia zvezda* report of the statement consisted of a highly selective collection of excerpts which failed entirely to reflect the note of conciliation which the document as a whole projected. Instead they stressed the uncertainties that clouded the international horizon and the need for undiminished vigilance.

ventured open dissent from the government's arms control policy.[16]

During 1969 this rearguard sniping at the government's policy subsided somewhat, but a more positive strategy aimed at registering a pessimistic, and even alarmist, assessment of military needs took its place. Marshal Krylov's blistering assessment of American policy in the newspaper *Soviet Russia* on August 30, 1969, and Major General Lagovskiy's rationalization of the need for continued heavy outlays for defense in the newspaper *Red Star* some weeks later are cases in point.[17] One may even speculate that the heftiness of the military contingent on the Soviet negotiating team for SALT is a result of military activism on the issue, since it apparently registers the regime's concern to ensure military support for any actions taken.

Is this opposition of such proportions as to constitute a serious threat to the Soviet Union's current policy on arms control? The answer is probably no. The Soviet Union has committed itself to at least exploring the possibilities of a strategic arms limitation agreement with the United States. It has done so, moreover, after a long period of deliberation in which the leaders were no doubt subject to all the arguments and pressures that the press occasionally brings to the attention of outside observers.

Over the longer run, of course, the picture may change, and the balance of forces operating on the policy-makers may shift accordingly. If the talks pro-

[16] See Colonel E. Rybkin, *Kommunist vooruzhennykh sil*, no. 18 (September 1968); and Colonel V. Bondarenko, *Kommunist vooruzhennykh sil*, no. 23 (December 1968).

[17] September 25, 1969.

duce evidence that satisfactory results cannot be expected, some of the policy-makers may be encouraged to reassess their positions. In this event, the military opposition would have redeemed itself, for the awareness of factiousness in their military constituency would no doubt be a factor working to encourage the leaders to consider alternative courses of action.

## THE LEADERSHIP

All the considerations and conflicting pressures are brought to focus finally on the eleven men in the Politburo. Their capabilities, their political relationships, and, above all, the stability of the arrangements that enable them to act in common are obviously vital questions affecting Soviet policy on the arms control issue.

The record of the post-Khrushchev years provides mixed answers. The Soviet leadership has demonstrated reasonable efficiency in handling the affairs of government and in carrying out an ambitious program of military development. It has obviously had trouble in matching means to ends, particularly with respect to the allocation of resources to investment, and recent evidence suggests that it may be forced to back off from a number of the major goals of domestic policy to which it committed itself. In foreign affairs, however, it has managed to avoid major blunders, while demonstrating an increasingly effective ability to make its presence felt on issues affecting Soviet national interests. It is hard to give the leadership high marks for its handling of the Czechoslovak crisis, but it can at least be argued that the Soviet Union's position in the communist world is no worse than it was before.

17

One of the major weaknesses of the Soviet leadership is in the realm of decision-making; indeed, it has shown increasing signs of difficulty in this respect as it has moved beyond the stage where anti-Khrushchevism was a unifying principle that provided a rationale for action. It is difficult to make a negative case on this point, since the distinction between indecision and a deliberate decision not to act is often a matter of subjective judgment. But most observers would probably agree that the leadership's performance on such issues as the development and approval of the Five Year Plan and the decision to intervene in Czechoslovakia revealed more than the normal amount of difficulty in reaching agreement. At times, these problems have apparently produced deadlocks, and even breakdowns of discipline, within the leadership. The rumors that Kosygin might resign, the attack on the leadership's handling of the Middle East crisis by Moscow Party Secretary Yegorichev at the June 1967 Plenum, and the challenge of official decisions on agriculture by Politburo member Polyanskii in his *Kommunist* article in the fall of 1967 are cases in point. The impression created by these and other events is that the leadership has often stalled and procrastinated on hard issues, and has preferred to base its policies on considerations of expediency and the lowest common denominator of the various personal and institutional interests represented in the ruling group.

The Soviet leadership appears to have had great difficulty in reaching a decision to accept strategic arms limitation talks with the United States. The first public reactions to the invitation extended by President Johnson in his State of the Union Message in January

1967 betrayed lack of preparation, at least, and possibly disagreement over how to respond. Kosygin, at his February 1967 press conference in London, took a noncommittal position on the question of the proposed talks, but he emphasized that the Soviet Union regarded ABMs as "defensive" in nature and, hence, not a disturbing element in the arms balance. *Pravda*, however, in reporting the press conference, represented Kosygin as having taken a more positive attitude toward talks on both "offensive" and "defensive" strategic weapons. This was followed by reports leaked to the western press that Soviet officials were embarrassed by the *Pravda* article, and that a new article, laying down the regime's negative position regarding the ABM side of the proposed agenda, would be forthcoming. In fact, this statement was never issued. Apart from this evidence of disarray at the beginning, the long period of official silence that followed was itself testimony to indecision within the leadership. Some eighteen months elapsed before the Soviet decision was finally announced in Gromyko's speech to the Supreme Soviet on June 27, 1968. It seems safe to assume that the issue was in the balance during much of this period and that the final decision turned on a close vote.

There is little evidence to indicate where the individual leaders stand on the strategic arms limitation issue. While all the leaders have probably given formal assent to the present policy, the mandate they have given is most likely a tentative one. However persuasive the reasons for an agreement might seem to some leaders, the considerations others find to counsel caution will also carry considerable weight. For some leaders, the potential benefits, particularly budgetary ones, may out-weigh the dangers they no doubt see in lowering their psychological guard against the United States. Others in the leadership who champion the causes of the military and party orthodoxy almost certainly weigh the balance of dangers and benefits differently.

The Soviet Union's scope for maneuver and compromise in the talks will be constrained by the need to avoid actions that could be interpreted by the more suspicious and skeptical members of the leadership as detrimental to Soviet interests, or as evidence of weakness. Matters of image and prestige are likely to be of great importance. For example, the question of American willingness to acknowledge the Soviet Union as an equal in great-power relationships will almost certainly be regarded by the Soviet Union as a precondition for substantive agreements.

The Soviet Union is entering the strategic arms limitation talks with the United States under mixed compulsions and constraints. There are compelling reasons why the Soviet Union should seek ways of moderating the arms race, and persuasive reasons why it should move cautiously toward that end. There are strong political forces in the regime favoring the movement toward a moderation of the arms race, and other forces opposing it, fearful that the momentum of the talks may propel the leaders into unsound agreements. The Soviet Union's decision to enter the talks does not resolve these contradictions; the policy-makers will continue to operate under intense and conflicting pressures throughout the negotiations. But the decision does indicate that the incentives for talks are presently stronger than the inhibitions opposing them.

# 2

## Soviet-American Strategic Relations:
## Implications for Arms Control

### INTRODUCTION

WE ENTER THE DECADE of the 1970s at a crucial time in Soviet-American strategic and political relations. For the first time both superpowers are strategic equals; both are undertaking or considering new and massive arms programs; both seem aware of the potentially destabilizing characteristics of these new weapons; and, finally, both are engaged in the strategic arms limitation talks.

In this chapter, we shall examine how this dilemma is seen from Moscow and analyze the relationship between Soviet strategic policy and arms control. How are Soviet arms control attitudes and policies influenced by (1) the Soviet-American strategic interaction? (2) the developments of defense technology and its pressures on policy choices? (3) Soviet perceptions of the United States? and (4) internal Soviet policy factors and values relevant to arms control interests?

The history of Soviet policy on disarmament and arms control is full of contradictions and marked by distrust, hostility, and misunderstanding. The motives for Soviet statements on the subject defy clear understanding, and the statements themselves rarely inspire western confidence. Soviet leaders have generally preached disarmament and peaceful coexistence, but at the same time they retain a militant ideology, an overwhelming reliance on their might of arms, and a deep distrust of western proposals on arms limitation. The confusion stems from a dualism in Soviet declaratory policy. On the one hand, the Bolsheviks initially rejected the desirability of disarmament since it would stabilize the international situation and hinder the spread of the revolutionary momentum. On the other hand, after Stalin came into power and after the revolutionary fervor was exhausted, the Soviet Union needed to assure other powers of its "peaceful" designs and international legitimacy, and so it initiated a massive propaganda drive on behalf of disarmament. Thus, while Lenin had urged his followers to "let the hypocritical or sentimental bourgeoisie dream disarmament . . . we must strive not for disarmament but for universal and popular armament,"[1] his followers tempered such ideological imperatives with declarations of peace, coexistence, and disarmament.[2] This combination of extreme militancy and avowed reasonableness has created misgivings among many in the West about the

[1] V. I. Lenin, *Sochineniia* (Works), vol. 8 (2d ed.; Moscow: Gosizdat, 1926–32), p. 395.

[2] A most recent collection of such formal Soviet disarmament proposals is contained in *50 let borby SSSR za razoruzheniie, 1917–67* (Fifty Years of Soviet Struggle for Disarmament, 1917–1967) (Moscow: Izdatel'stvo "Nauka," 1967).

real intentions and objectives of the Soviet leadership. It has also eroded credibility in Soviet statements as a useful guide to Soviet policy objectives and intentions.

If the West has been skeptical about Soviet avowals for peace and disarmament, how then have generations of Soviet leaders perceived western intentions and objectives vis-à-vis the Soviet Union? The Soviet Union entered the international arena as a revolutionary, militant, and expansionist state whose formal ideologies aimed at the subversion and eventual destruction of western capitalistic systems. Moreover, the Soviet Union grew and developed behind punitive *cordons sanitaire* and "capitalist encirclements," in the face of western policies of "roll back" and containment and asserted western strategic superiority. This combination of militant ideology and perceptions of a very hostile international environment has instilled in Soviet leaders a kind of political paranoia and a deep distrust of the West. It has also engendered a strong expectation of threat and a corresponding reliance on their own defense capabilities. Generations of Soviet leaders were raised on the Leninist philosophy of a basic "Bolshevik belief that enemies strive not merely to contain the Party . . . but rather to annihilate it."[3] Thus Stalin spoke of basic contradictions between the two camps, capitalist and socialist, and concluded that the "essence of the question" is "who will defeat whom?"[4] Khrushchev maintained that "the imperialists walk

[3] Nathan Leites, *A Study of Bolshevism* (Glencoe, Ill.: The Free Press, 1953), p. 8.

[4] *Report to the Fourteenth Conference of the Russian Communist Party*, May 9, 1925.

around the fence of the socialist countries like hungry wolves around a sheep pen."[5] He also warned that "some people watch us with greedy eyes and think how they can disarm us. But what would happen if we disarmed? We would certainly be torn to pieces."[6] Brezhnev alluded to the "dangerous intrigues by the enemies of peace,"[7] while Shelepin warned that "the Soviet Union has no right to ignore the constantly threatening danger of a new military attack by the predatory imperialists."[8]

The Soviet vision of a hostile international environment has strongly influenced Soviet policy and strategy. It has contributed to a sense of primary need for: military readiness and strength; national priorities in which the defense sector almost invariably comes first; internal vigilance and mobilization of resources and manpower in anticipation of external threat; and, finally, a pervasive mistrust of negotiated agreements which might hinder the pursuit of optimal defense interests.

As long as Soviet leaders considered their defense capabilities inferior to those of the West and inadequate for their basic security and political interests, they refrained from seriously considering strategic arms limitation agreements. It is postulated here that an indispensable precondition for Soviet willingness to

[5] N. Khrushchev, Radio Moscow, August 24, 1959.

[6] N. Khrushchev in 1955, cited in R. Kolkowicz, "The Role of Disarmament in Soviet Policy," *The Prospects for Arms Control*, ed. James E. Dougherty (New York: Macfadden-Bartell Corp., 1965), p. 95.

[7] Radio Moscow, July 3, 1965.

[8] *Pravda*, July 25, 1965.

consider strategic arms control was the achievement
of some form of strategic equality with the United
States, and that this goal has recently been reached.

## FROM STRATEGIC INFERIORITY TO PARITY

Soviet attitudes toward arms control are intimately
related to several important political and military considerations: the absolute and relative levels of Soviet
strategic capabilities vis-à-vis those of the United States;
the policy styles of several Soviet leaders; Soviet perceptions of threat levels created by the U.S. adversary;
and certain institutional politics within the Soviet
bureaucracies.

### Evolution of Soviet Military Policy

The evolution of Soviet military policy since the end
of World War II can be schematically divided into
three periods which correspond approximately to the
regimes and policy styles of Stalin, Khrushchev, and
Brezhnev-Kosygin. The three periods are also roughly
parallel to some major political, military, and technological changes.

*Stalin: Persistence of Orthodoxy.* The period from
the end of World War II to the death of Stalin in 1953
was characterized by a basic reliance on massive conventional forces, deployed in an active defense posture
with a narrow, continental mission. This military policy
derived from Stalin's *Principles of Warfare*, which were
based largely on his experiences during the war.
Though modern military weapons and equipment were
being introduced into the Soviet military establishment,
Stalin continued to force his strategists to "look back"

to the successful Russo-German war and to draw theoretical and practical lessons of warfare from that period. Stalin had initiated a massive crash program for the development of atomic weapons soon after the war, yet he failed to consider the radical implications of such weapons for the nature of future warfare, strategy, and politics. As one Soviet military analyst recently suggested, "Stalin did not consider the atomic bomb as a radically different weapon," and he continued to view his military problems in the light of his past experiences.[9]

*Khrushchev: Militant Style, Flexible Policy.* Stalin left to his successors a host of complex problems that had existed throughout his rule. Yet before his followers could seriously begin the necessary process of modernization and reform, they had to settle the political succession struggles in the party. Only after Khrushchev ousted Malenkov from his high positions in the party and government in 1955 and had destroyed the myth of the infallibility of Stalin in 1956 were Soviet strategists and analysts able to undertake the reform of strategic doctrines and policies.

In the decade after Stalin's death, Soviet military policy underwent far-reaching reappraisals and innovations. Military technology and weaponry were modernized; the massive conventional forces were gradually reduced by more than half; and strategic doctrine and policy were sharply modified. Moreover, the Soviet Union's political influence and role around the globe were enhanced and its commitments expanded. After

[9] For details, see R. Kolkowicz, "Soviet Strategic Debates: An Important Addendum" (P-2936; Santa Monica, Cal.: The RAND Corporation, July 1964).

an initial period of ambiguity (1953–60), Soviet military posture and strategic doctrine were formalized: the newly created Strategic Rocket Forces, the Air Defense Forces, and the expanded subsurface navy were given a global mission of deterrence, while the sharply reduced conventional forces were assigned a smaller role in the continental, defensive posture, largely as an auxiliary to the strategic forces.[10]

The new strategic doctrine and posture reflected Khrushchev's views that a future war, however initiated, would rapidly become an all-out nuclear exchange, thus necessitating reliable strategic deterrent capabilities and only marginal conventional forces. This new Soviet strategic doctrine, formally announced in January 1960, was strikingly similar to the "massive retaliation" principles advocated and then abandoned by the United States in the 1950s. An underlying premise of the new strategy was Khrushchev's belief that nuclear war had become politically useless, since there would be no victors and the damage inflicted would be so devastating that organized society would cease to exist. Khrushchev arrived at this position only gradually. In 1954 he had maintained that in the event of a nuclear war the "imperialists will choke on it and it will end up in a catastrophe for the imperialist world."[11] In 1955 he still subscribed to the view that "we cannot be intimidated by fables that in the event of a new world war civilization will perish."[12] In 1956 he began to hedge, stating that "war is not fatal-

---

[10] See R. Kolkowicz, *The Soviet Military and the Communist Party* (Princeton, N.J.: Princeton University Press, 1967), pp. 150–73.

[11] *Pravda*, June 13, 1954.

[12] *Pravda*, March 27, 1955.

istically inevitable,"[13] and by 1958 he reversed his past positions asserting that "a future war ... would cause immeasurable harm to all mankind."[14]

Having rejected the idea of the political utility of nuclear war, Khrushchev also rejected the idea of local wars and limited nuclear war,[15] since according to his new strategic doctrine, these would rapidly become major nuclear wars. For ideological and tactical reasons he retained the formulas about "wars of national liberation" being "just" and meriting the support of the Soviet government. It is rather unlikely that he actually contemplated any direct involvement of Soviet forces on behalf of such "just" wars, given the rather inadequate size and quality of his conventional forces.

While moderating the archaic dictums of Soviet ideology in accord with the basic political changes caused by the emergence of missile-nuclear weapons, Khrushchev nevertheless continued to pursue a very vigorous policy of military buildup. He sought to avoid war or a major confrontation with the United States, and Soviet leaders continued to talk of peaceful coexistence with the West. But, at the same time, the

[13] TASS, February 14, 1956.

[14] Radio Budapest, April 3, 1958.

[15] Typical of Khrushchev's views on the disutility of limited war "with which the imperialists want to suppress the national liberation movements and do away with governments which do not suit them. . . . Should such wars break out, they could soon grow into a world war." TASS, December 5, 1967. For evidence of Soviet military pressure to reverse this policy, see Kolkowicz, "Soviet Strategic Debates."

Soviet defense industry began to produce strategic missiles, the Red Army underwent a massive reorganization program intended to increase its firepower and mobility, and the emphasis of Soviet strategic doctrine was shifted from conventional to strategic missile-nuclear forces.

When the U–2 episode unmasked the superficiality of Soviet-American peaceful coexistence and exposed anew the deep-seated distrust that underlay it, Khrushchev abandoned the role of peace-loving statesman and turned to threatening the world with aggression. The Soviets shrewdly exploited the highly publicized western miscalculations of the number of deployed Soviet ICBMs, seizing upon the so-called "missile gap" as an opportunity to extract political gains, to maintain the initiative in international affairs, and to make negotiations on disarmament less desirable.

When the missile gap was exposed as myth in 1961, the West began to make more realistic estimates of Soviet strategic capabilities. The United States began to increase its missile production, massively raising western strategic capabilities, and leaving no doubt as to where the strategic balance of power lay. The Soviet leaders then had to face some hard choices: first, they could deny the revised western estimates of Soviet strategic capabilities and insist on their nuclear superiority; second, they could engage in a large-scale arms race, trying to keep pace with, or even to outdistance, the West in the production of strategic weapons; third, they could attempt stopgap measures in order to minimize the growing preponderance of U.S. strategic missile forces; or fourth, they could resign themselves to being an inferior military-strategic power and shift from a hard, militant line to a more conciliatory line in East-West relations.

In retrospect it seems that Khrushchev, consciously perhaps, embarked on a policy of gradually ascending risks and costs. Because of the limitations of the Soviet economy (his ambitious Seven-Year Plan, aimed at the domestic sector of the economy, was running into difficulties), Khrushchev viewed a full-scale armaments race with the West as the least desirable option, and he did not attempt it. Presumably he also understood the futility of such a move, since the United States could easily surpass any increment in Soviet strategic capabilities. For a time, the Soviet leaders experimented with the first and third options. At the Twenty-second Party Congress in the fall of 1961, Marshal Malinovskii still boasted of the powerful might of Soviet missiles; later the Soviets declared that the superior quality of Soviet weapons (i.e., their enormous destructive power) counterbalanced the quantity of U.S. missiles. This was empty boasting. The next Soviet ploy, aimed at achieving some sort of parity in deterrence, was by far the most risky. This effort was culminated by the attempt to place offensive missiles in Cuba. When this venture failed, Khrushchev started to pursue the fourth option —a search for détente with the West.

Khrushchev's policies were based on beliefs of "tolerable" actions, on certain assumptions of western constraints on Soviet initiatives, and on assumptions regarding the desirability and utility of exploiting strategic power for political purposes. Western political analysts generally agree that the basic aspects of Soviet foreign and strategic policies at that time included the following: an assumption that the United States would be very reluctant to go to war with the Soviet Union, unless, of course, it was dangerously provoked; a belief that the United States had rejected nuclear war as an instrument of policy; a relative Soviet disinterest in the activities of smaller countries, which was in part the result of a central preoccupation with the United States; and a belief that the balance of world power was shifting to the advantage of the socialist camp.

In sum, Khrushchev's policies were designed to keep the West deterred by asserting Soviet strategic superiority, and to retain and consolidate Soviet gains since World War II. At home, he sought to generate an ambitious economic resurgence which would satisfy rising consumer demands and overcome the perennial weaknesses of the economy. The result of his policies was disappointing—the West tested the credibility of his nuclear diplomacy and clearly showed the world the hollowness of Soviet militancy. Within the communist bloc, the former satellites pressed for greater freedom and autonomy and obtained a large measure of both, and China turned from an ally into an enemy. Domestically, his sweeping reforms confused the planners and alienated the bureaucrats and most of the military and Soviet party leaders by undercutting their traditional powers and privileges.[16] Khrushchev tried to accomplish too much with too little, hoping to fill the gap between capabilities and objectives with a deceitful, verbal overkill. His policy reflected his overcommit-

---

[16] For details, see R. Kolkowicz, "Die Position der Sowjetarmee vor und nach dem Sturz Chruschtschows," *Osteuropa*, October 1966, pp. 671–84.

ment to domestic, intrabloc, and international objectives; his modus operandi became a hit-and-run process, which tried to accommodate some objectives at one time and others at another time. It was a daring, nerve-racking venture that failed.

*Brezhnev-Kosygin: Pragmatic Style, Militant Policy.* The new regime, headed by Premier Alexei Kosygin and Party Secretary Leonid Brezhnev, was faced with a serious situation brought about by Khrushchev's methods and the substance of his policies. First, the credibility of Soviet military capabilities had been severely undermined; such disbelief was considered a dangerous precedent which might embolden a potential opponent to challenge the Soviet Union. Second, Khrushchev's erratic and "harebrained" diplomatic behavior had not only disturbed international politics and motivated the United States to remain prepared and militant, but it also had compromised Soviet policy and international influence. Third, his overcommitment to varied policy objectives had often negated planning policies, which were convulsed by massive and sudden "grand designs." To the new regime, the antidote to this malaise of bombast, irresponsible claims, erratic political behavior, and confusing crash planning seemed to be pragmatism and the establishment of credibility through the attainment of conspicuous capabilities to match objectives and declaratory policy.

The new regime's policy formula indeed struck this note: "We are striving to make our diplomacy vigorous and active and at the same time we exhibit flexibility and caution."[17] It was to be a policy of "opposing

---

[17] General Secretary of CPSU L. Brezhnev in *Pravda*, September 30, 1965.

aggressive imperialist circles without allowing itself any sabre-rattling or irresponsible talk," based on a "business-like approach" to a new pragmatism in which "a mere bookish knowledge of Marxism does not supply the confidence possible for working policy."[18]

The policy was, therefore, one of restraint, prudence, and continuing détente, based on a deterrent relation with the United States and on pragmatic, balanced economic planning at home. It could be described as a "speak-softly-while-you-are-getting-a-big-stick" policy. The regime's appraisal of the nature of U.S. strategic deterrence convinced them of the need to avoid provocations that would lead the superior adversary to war, or situations that could escalate into a major war, and either-or situations in which the alternatives would be war or severe concessions.

Though the new regime significantly transformed the method and style of Soviet policy, it did retain at least two of Khrushchev's underlying assumptions regarding the political and strategic environment of the Soviet state: (1) nuclear war would be a catastrophe for both the East and the West; and (2) a policy of détente and nuclear deterrence is essential, since it is the primary mechanism for preventing unprovoked nuclear attacks and for regulating the whole range of Soviet-American relations. This policy of détente and deterrence, however, was not seen as a constraint on political or military initiatives in areas that were presumed to be of less than vital interest to the other superpowers, as long as they were conducted according to the "rules of the game."

[18] Editorial in the party's main theoretical organ, *Kommunist*, no. 12, August 1965.

Nor was this new attitude of prudence and pragmatism to prevent the new regime from undertaking ambitious defense programs. The new leaders were clearly aware of the marked Soviet strategic inferiority vis-à-vis the United States. They also realized the fallacy of their predecessor's strategic doctrine which rested on an all-or-nothing proposition regarding nuclear war. Such a rigid doctrine had deprived the Soviet Union of military flexibility and the necessary range of options for dealing with conflicts involving conventional weapons. Consequently, the new regime embarked on a policy aimed at accelerated programs for the production of offensive and defensive strategic weapons, while simultaneously upgrading the role and mission of the conventional forces. As a result, Soviet military capabilities in the late 1960s grew dramatically. The Soviets obtained near parity with the United States in offensive strategic weapons, and they embarked on an impressive building program for the navy and air forces.[19]

## Strategic Asymmetry and Symmetry

A remarkable aspect in the evolution of Soviet and American strategies and capabilities lies in the fact that until very recently these two powers were in an asymmetrical relationship, or out of phase with each other. Only in the past two or three years have their capabilities, postures, and doctrines achieved a rough symmetry. It is assumed here that this variance between the two powers strongly affected Soviet attitudes toward a wide range of issues and policies, including

[19] See appendix A.

34

their assessments of threat levels and of the utility of arms control.

The evolution of American and Soviet strategic policies in the past two decades is illustrated briefly below.

| *United States* | *Soviet Union* |
|---|---|

### 1949–1954

| United States | Soviet Union |
|---|---|
| Rearming | Consolidating World War II gains |
| Containment of Russia | |
| Engagement in Europe and Asia | Defensive, continental posture |
| Global posture | |

### 1955–1960

| United States | Soviet Union |
|---|---|
| Massive retaliation doctrine | Ambiguous doctrine |
| Reliance on strategic forces | Reliance on conventional forces |
| Militant | Ambiguous posture |

### 1961–1964

| United States | Soviet Union |
|---|---|
| Evolution of deterrence theory and flexible response capabilities | "Massive retaliation" doctrine |
| Seaching for strategic parity and superiority | Inflexible posture |
| | Strategically inferior |

### 1965–1969

| United States | Soviet Union |
|---|---|
| Deterrent capability | Deterrent capability |
| Flexible response and global posture | Flexible response and global posture |
| Strategic parity | Strategic parity |

Soviet strategic doctrine and capabilities appear to have lagged behind those of the United States by about five years. The United States and its allies, for example, created a regional defense alliance system in Europe in 1949 (NATO), and the Soviet Union followed suit in 1955 (the Warsaw Pact). The United States adopted the doctrine of massive retaliation around 1955, and then rejected it several years later.

The periods after 1960 bear a closer look. In the first half of the decade, the United States further developed the theory of deterrence and strove to retain a sizable strategic superiority over the Soviet Union. Having abandoned its massive retaliation doctrine, the United States embarked on a program of creating an all-purpose, flexible response force that would be able to deal with conflicts in remote areas. During the same period, the Soviet Union adopted a strategic doctrine akin to massive retaliation and sharply reduced the size and role of its conventional forces. Soviet strategic doctrine resulted in a rigid, inflexible posture for its armed forces, and despite Soviet declaratory statements, the country was strategically inferior to the United States.

Since 1964 the United States has strengthened and improved its deterrent capabilities and generally adhered to a flexible response doctrine. Defense capabilities reached the designed ceilings and U.S. political and military policies remained globally committed. During this period the Soviet Union came into phase militarily with the United States. It also adopted a flexible response doctrine, achieved strategic equality with the United States, and placed its strategic and conventional capabilities in a global configuration.

Several implications can be derived from the asymmetry and symmetry in Soviet-American strategic doctrines and capabilities. First, modern defense technology determines to a large extent the kind of strategic doctrines and policies that will be adopted by the superpowers. Thus, technology seems to have a leveling effect which subsumes political, ideological, and social differences in various political systems. Second, western strategic doctrines have had an "educative" effect on Soviet political and military leaders, persuading the latter to exchange their own ideas and programs for "capitalistic" and "bourgeois" ones. Third, economic-social systems less advanced than that of the United States can, when national priorities are adjusted, create massive and sophisticated arsenals of advanced weapons and technologies.

In a more pragmatic fashion, one can derive other important implications. First, claims to superpower status require actual military and technological capabilities in their support. Previous inflated Soviet claims to such alleged capabilities were bluntly discounted by the West, and in the process Soviet credibility was eroded. Moreover, inflated Soviet claims generated unanticipated and countervailing results: having been threatened by Soviet verbal overkill, the United States undertook crash armament programs by which it quickly outdistanced the Soviet Union. The Soviets learned a dear lesson and undertook their own crash armament programs. Second, having finally achieved strategic equality at some cost, the Soviets created a new psychological threat for some westerners who became used to the notion that only western strategic superiority could ensure their basic interests as well as general international stability. Many in the West now feel the need for a new armament cycle to outdistance the Soviets once more. Some even consider such an action-reaction cycle to be anti-Soviet weapon. Their argument is that the West can "bleed" the Soviet system by forcing it to keep up with U.S. arms programs, which presumably would strain the Soviet economy to the breaking point.

## Adversary Perception and Strategy

An important aspect of the deterrence relationship is that the deterred adversaries are presumed to understand and abide by the new "calculus of terror," the implicit and explicit rules of the game of deterrence. Such concepts as signaling, adversary perceptions, escalatory levels, first strike, second strike, nuclear pause, assured destruction, damage limitation, catalytic war, and the like, have been widely embraced by strategic and policy communities of the West. Since a deterrent relationship is seen as a "balance of terror," it is crucial that the balance is not upset by misunderstood signals, misinterpreted intent, and action based on faulty adversary perception. Vital questions in this context are: How do the adversaries read the presumed rules of the game? Do they understand them in a similar manner? In other words, what is the nature of the adversary, and how do perceptions of the adversary influence strategic doctrines and policies?

Most western studies of Soviet strategic schools or groups generally divide them into traditionalists and radicals.[20] The former are assumed to reflect the biases and institutional interests of the conventional armed forces, while the latter reflect the interests of the strategic

[20] See, for example, T. W. Wolfe's *Soviet Strategy at the Crossroads* (Cambridge, Mass.: Harvard University Press, 1964).

and more technologically oriented branches of the armed forces. This typology is based on evidence provided by public Soviet "strategic debates" during the early and middle 1960s. However, the typology is rather narrowly derived and is too intimately bound to institutional military interests.

For the sake of simplicity, we can divide Soviet strategic views and positions into two broader categories, the conservative and pragmatic. This informal typology is based on analyses of Soviet conditions and essentially describes the broad outlooks of the two groups. Listed below schematically are the positions taken by members of the two groups on specific issues and values.

| *Conservatives* | *Pragmatists* |
| --- | --- |
| High threat estimates | Moderate threat estimates |
| Adversary image: militant, threatening | Adversary image: selective |
| Demand high defense budgets | Satisfied with party-established defense budget |
| See utility in nuclear war | Deny utility of nuclear war |
| Urge strategic superiority | Desire parity |
| Dissatisfied with deterrence only | Support a deterrence policy |
| Prefer offensive strategy | Desire an offensive-defensive strategy |
| Against arms control | Support arms control |

The two groups comprise people from the military establishment and the party leadership. Their policy positions and general world views tend to reflect opera-

tional needs (ongoing political maneuvering to maxi-
mize political or institutional interests), as well as basic
attitudes and biases. While specific, articulated conservative or pragmatic attitudes are frequently dictated
by specific policy phases of the Soviet Union (conciliatory or militant), at other times sharp disagreements
emerge from various institutional or political spokesmen
which contradict state policy and reflect actual expres-
sions of dissent.

Let us briefly examine some details of this postulated
conservative-pragmatic interaction in the Soviet Union
and seek to discern evolving Soviet images of war,
strategy, and arms control.

The earliest public expression of conservative-pragmatic disagreements since Stalin's death appeared in
1953 when Premier Malenkov struck a tone of reasonableness and moderation with reference to foreign
affairs and proposed curtailment of military allocations.
The following spring he went even further by introducing a nondogmatic view of international relations,
suggesting that a thermonuclear war would result in
a "new world slaughter . . . [and] would mean the
destruction of world civilization."[21] This position constituted a sharp departure from traditional Soviet views
on war. It also challenged the interests and positions
of the conservatives in the party and military.

The threatened conservatives challenged Malenkov
publicly, forced him to change his position, and finally
ousted him from his high governmental and party positions.[22] Soon after Malenkov's ouster in 1955, the con-

[21] *Pravda*, March 13, 1954.
[22] See Kolkowicz, *The Soviet Military*, pp. 105–13.

servatives formally re-established their views and policies. Ranking party leaders asserted that "no matter how severe the consequences of atomic war, they cannot be identified with the fall of world civilization."[23] They also condemned views which maintained that "inasmuch as both East and West possess hydrogen weapons, the possibility of a thermonuclear war is automatically excluded." Such views, they stated, "can in fact lull the vigilance of the peoples."[24] Politburo member Molotov brutally asserted that in the event of a thermonuclear war "what will perish will not be world civilizations . . . but the decaying [capitalist] social system with its imperialist core soaked in blood."[25] The conservatives also re-established the primacy of defense priorities and readjusted budgetary allocations to that end.[26]

One of the strongest champions of conservatism in the early and middle 1950s was Khrushchev, who, in the process, gained full political power in the government and the party. As the decade wore on, however, there emerged a fuller appreciation of the implications of a nuclear war conducted with intercontinental ballistic missiles. A better perception of the delicate balance of terror and of the deterrence relationship between the two major powers had its impacts. The vast expense of the new nuclear technology began to conflict with other high-priority objectives within the domestic programs.

By the early 1960s, especially after the abortive

[23] *Kommunist*, no. 4 (April 1965), pp. 16–17.
[24] Defense Minister Nikolai Bulganin, *Pravda*, January 1, 1956.
[25] Politburo member V. Molotov, *Pravda*, February 9, 1955.
[26] For details, see Kolkowicz, *The Soviet Military*, pp. 105–50.

Cuban missile venture, Khrushchev became a proselytizing pragmatist. He firmly embraced the new gospel of détente, deterrence, and negotiations. Ironically, he found himself in a position similar to that of the hapless Malenkov a decade earlier. Asserting that "of late, a certain relaxation of tension has become apparent in international affairs," Khrushchev suggested that "the tasks of the [defense industry] could be solved more successfully with less expenditure." He now rejected the conservatives' traditional demands for subordinating "the needs of the stomach" (i.e., domestic and consumer-oriented priorities) to those of defense: "The highest calling of Soviet man, his primary duty, consists of creating and amassing wealth for the country, for a better life." He argued that revolutionary "passion is a fine thing, of course, but after the passion we must tackle the economy . . . so that we can eat well, have good housing." This would be "far better than merely revolutionary passion." Having thus established his preferences for new social priorities, Khrushchev went on to propose reduced defense budgets, maintaining that "the defense of the country is at a suitable level," and he proposed a new policy line aimed at "solving controversial international problems through negotiations."[27]

These policies and attitudes of Khrushchev had a shock effect on the conservatives, especially among the military. Khrushchev had denigrated the role and uses of conventional forces; he adhered to an obsolescent strategic doctrine akin to massive retaliation; his new political moderation vitiated much of the necessary

[27] See *Ibid.*, appendix G, pp. 383–85.

rationale for high defense priorities; and he resorted to selective adversary perceptions, distinguishing between "sane forces in the USA" and "aggressive military circles."[28]

Like Malenkov before him, Khrushchev's pragmatic attitudes and policies alienated the conservatives and unified them for the purpose of ousting him from power. Soon after ousting Khrushchev, which was accomplished with remarkable smoothness and swiftness,[29] the conservatives celebrated their victory in a public outburst of self-congratulation and vindictiveness. Summarily rejecting most of Khrushchev's policies and views, they asserted that "the current international situation is characterized by a sharpening of tension and increased danger of war."[30] They maintained that the primary consideration of the party is "its sacred duty to strengthen the defense power of the USSR," which it regards as "the most important function of the Soviet state."[31] They warned that "we have no right to forget the continuous dangers which threaten us in the form of a potential military attack by the imperialist aggressors."[32] As for Khrushchev's "goulash communism" and his domestic priorities, these now received short shrift: "It would be most incorrect to see as the central purpose of Communism mainly the satisfaction of the 'needs of the stomach.' "[33]

The Brezhnev-Kosygin regime seems to have em-

[28] *Ibid.*, pp. 150–73.
[29] See Kolkowicz, "Die Position der Sowjetarmee."
[30] *Kommunist*, no. 7 (May 1965).
[31] *Ibid.*, editorial.
[32] A. Shelepin, *Pravda*, July 25, 1965.
[33] *Pravda*, May 17, 1965.

braced the view that "the Soviet Union has no right to ignore the constantly threatening danger of a new military attack by the predatory imperialists"[34] and that, accordingly, "the Soviet government is devoting untiring attention to the further strengthening of the country's defense capabilities."[35] This view was reiterated by Brezhnev who maintained that "history has taught us that the stronger our army is, the more watchful we are, the stronger the peace on our frontiers. . . . We have learned that well."[36]

And, indeed, as we can judge with the benefit of hindsight, the new regime embarked on a massive, sustained, and orderly program for upgrading Soviet defense capabilities to attain strategic parity with the United States. They also strengthened their conventional forces and assigned them a new, more active role. The defense budgets continued to be increased yearly and the political influence of the military rose considerably.[37]

By the mid-1960s, however, the conservatives, mainly in the military, felt themselves threatened anew by certain heretical views and policy proposals. The dissatisfaction with the new regime built up in the same manner as it did in the Khrushchev era. Both regimes came into power with the assistance, or at least tacit acquiescence, of the conservatives. Once in power, they had to satisfy many of the demands of the conservatives, but they found themselves pressed by a variety of con-

[34] Defense Minister A. Grechko, Radio Moscow, February 23, 1968.
[35] A. Shelepin, *Pravda*, July 25, 1965.
[36] Radio Moscow, July 3, 1965.
[37] See appendix A.

flicting demands and claims from many sectors of society and interest groups. In order to strike a workable balance among the demands on resources, priorities, and influence, both regimes resorted to a policy of partial accommodation to the strongest claimants and, in the process, alienated most of them.

The military's dissatisfaction with the Brezhnev-Kosygin regime was caused by a number of factors: the regime's emerging moderate and conciliatory foreign policy; the attempts to subordinate strategic doctrine and policy authority to party initiative and control; the alleged inadequacy of allocations to the defense sector; and the emerging economic pragmatism in the party's planning policies.

The conservatives, largely from the military, embarked on a sustained campaign to impress the regime with the urgency, cogency, and rationality of their views and demands. At the center of the conservative position were: assessments of high threat levels from the United States (and later China); the desire to reinvigorate Soviet society, institutions, and its leaders with conservative zeal; the rejection of dangerous "fatalistic" doctrines in the Soviet Union; and, last but not least, the desire to further the institutional interests of the military and the conservatives.

The pragmatists who have earned the wrath of the conservatives include numerous prominent Soviet personalities, presumably including Premier Kosygin. Their arguments are not based on antiregime or anticommunist principles. Rather, their positions and arguments seem to derive from a more pragmatic and prudent assessment of the opportunities, risks, and costs facing Soviet political and military policies at present.

A prominent Soviet strategist, for example, stated in 1965 that "in our time there is no more dangerous illusion than the idea that thermonuclear war can still serve as an instrument of politics; that it is possible to achieve political aims through the use of nuclear power, and at the same time survive; and that it is possible to find acceptable forms of nuclear war."[38]

The conservatives vigorously attacked this heretical position maintaining that "an a priori rejection of the possibility of victory is harmful" because it leads to a "moral disarmament . . . fatalism and passivity. It is necessary to wage a struggle against such views." They asserted that a nuclear war does not necessarily pose "a threat to physical survival of nations and states" and that it is very important to impress upon the Soviet people "the possibilities of conducting a victorious nuclear missile war."[39]

Another aspect of the pragmatic-conservative debate deals with the concept of strategic superiority. "Superiority has become a concept which has no bearing on war. No superiority can save the aggressor from retaliation. Any efforts of an aggressor to achieve relative nuclear superiority are neutralized in advance by the fact that the other side possesses absolute power which guarantees the destruction of the aggressor. . . ."[40]

Compare the above with the following: "The stern

[38] General N. Talenskii, "Reflecting on the Last War," *International Affairs* (Moscow), no. 5 (May 1965), p. 23.

[39] See R. Kolkowicz, "The Red 'Hawks' on the Rationality of Nuclear War" (RM-4899; Santa Monica, Cal.: The RAND Corporation, 1966).

[40] G. Gerasimov, *International Affairs* (Moscow), no. 5 (May 1966), p. 28.

dialectic of [military] development consists in the fact that the struggle for superiority must be waged incessantly. Any weakening of effort in this field, any excessive self-admiration because of success achieved"[41] can only lead to failure.

Typical of the range of formal disagreements between the conservatives and the pragmatists on the utility of arms control is the following. Foreign Minister Gromyko maintains that "only ignorant people or simple adventurists fail to realize what an armed conflict between the two social systems would mean. The world long ago reached the stage when the continuation of the arms race became madness."[42] A typical conservative rejoinder asserts that "we cannot agree with the view that disarmament can be achieved as a result of peaceful negotiations . . . by representatives of opposing social systems." The spokesman maintains that "quite to the contrary, it can only be achieved as a result of active struggle by the revolutionary forces in the imperialist countries" with the support of the socialist world. Thus, "any other concept about the path for the achievement of disarmament is an illusion." The conservative prescription is that until such a future situation prevails, "it is the primary task of the socialist countries to strengthen their armed forces and increase their capabilities and their readiness."[43]

The conservative-pragmatic dichotomy reflects, there-

[41] V. Bondarenko, "Military-Technological Superiority—A Most Important Factor in the Reliable Defense of the Country," *Kommunist vooruzhennykh sil*, no. 17 (September 1966).

[42] Speech at the U.N. General Assembly, October 3, 1968.

[43] Colonel E. Rybkin, *Kommunist vooruzhennykh sil*, no. 18 (September 1968).

fore, different views of the strategic and political possibilities of the state and different conclusions about the implications of policy alternatives. The conservatives seem to operate on the "worst plausible case" approach to interaction with the West. Their views are strikingly similar to those of the politically conservative and military-oriented groups in the West. On the other hand, the pragmatists approach the current strategic situation with a more prudent and concerned attitude. Their position is roughly similar to that of the more moderate strategic and political groups in the West. Curiously, the pragmatists' position is strikingly similar to that of former Defense Secretary McNamara in the final phase of his tenure in government. McNamara's position was that "we have both built up our 'second strike capability' to the point that a 'first strike capability' on either side has become unattainable." He stated further that neither a Soviet nor an American ABM system would provide an objectively greater measure of security because neither side "can attack the other without being destroyed in retaliation." And, finally, McNamara drew an ominous picture of the dynamics of the arms race: "There is a kind of mad momentum intrinsic to the development of all nuclear weaponry. If a system works—and works well—there is strong pressure from many directions to procure and deploy the weapon out of all proportions to the prudent level required."[44]

We can conclude from this brief examination that (1) the Soviet system is such that claimants to power must, at least for tactical purposes, stress orthodox

---

[44] Speech given in San Francisco, September 18, 1967, in *The Washington Post*, September 19, 1967.

conservative views and policies in order to defeat the opposition; (2) once in power, the leaders must seek a gradual reversal of attitudes and priorities from the conservative to a more pragmatic approach, in order to retain a workable internal and external balance of resources and allocations; (3) given the action-reaction strategic relation between the two opposing superpowers, and the internal "mad momentum of nuclear weaponry," it is very difficult and politically chancy to halt the escalation of the arms race; and (4) conservative attitudes and pressures in both systems tend to reinforce their respective threat assessment levels and to provide the driving dynamics for the arms race and for the related strategic doctrines and policies.

Let us return to the questions posed at the outset of this analysis. First, do the adversaries read the rules of the game of deterrence in a similar manner? The answer might be that similar groupings in the two diverse political systems read the rules in a similar manner, but formal policies derived from the readings of those rules will depend on which of the groupings dominates the particular political system. Second, how do perceptions of the adversary influence strategic doctrine and policy? Again, we may answer, that this would depend on which particular group does the assessing, and how such assessments are related to the evident dangers and limitation of possibilities inherent in a deterrent relationship based on a "balance of terror."

## STRATEGIC BALANCE AND ARMS CONTROL

We postulated earlier that a vital prerequisite for serious Soviet consideration of arms control was the achievement of strategic equality with the United States. We shall analyze here certain changes in Soviet attitudes toward the uses and role of strategic power and how this relates to arms control considerations.

## Political Considerations

The history of Soviet politics is largely that of a state at war or anticipating war. From its revolutionary origins, through the Stalinist dictatorship, and up to the past decade, Soviet policy was overwhelmingly motivated by the need to defend the country against numerous enemies and by the desire to expand its frontiers. Soviet policy, therefore, was based on a view of a hostile world and on a basic belief that "war is a continuation of politics." Moreover, ideological and doctrinal imperatives prevented the Soviet leaders from seeking lasting agreements with the capitalist countries, and this led, therefore, to an international relationship which involved various forms of armed truce or coexistence.

The introduction of strategic nuclear weapons changed this situation radically. Soviet leaders became convinced that nuclear war could not be a continuation of politics since it would destroy all belligerents. Since the Soviet leaders could not overcome this new constraint on their policy, and since they were interested in assuring their own security and policy interests in a nuclear context, they eagerly embraced the idea and reality of deterrence. Stable deterrence would not only protect them against unprovoked attacks, it would also formalize their superpower status in international affairs.

A deterrence relationship with the United States, however, created several new problems, as well as opportunities, for the Soviet leadership. The problems were related mainly to the initial inadequacy of the Soviet deterrent, which established a superior-inferior relationship vis-à-vis the United States. Moreover, a central characteristic of deterrence is that of a certain dualism among the deterred. Assuming that a deterrence relationship is one of a "balance of terror," it is vitally important that neither party undertake rash or threatening actions or policies, lest this vital balance become upset. This new phenomenon in international relations introduced a form of interdependence between the superpowers which necessitated circumspection and various forms of "signaling" and communication in their dealings. It also led to reappraisals of the political and military uses of strategic power. This Soviet reappraisal became manifest when the Soviet Union began to close the strategic gap, when its defense and policy interests seemed largely satisfied, and its traditional threat assessments became somewhat minimized.

The new Soviet attitudes toward strategic power derived from several considerations:

1. The strategic arms race is expensive and does not add much to the security of the Soviet Union. Having reached rough parity with the United States, the Soviet Union can gain little from a new arms-race spiral in which the United States could presumably outspend and outbuild the Soviet Union.

2. The political utility of strategic arms increments is not very significant, since, as the Soviets point out,

it cannot easily be applied to the vast number of non-nuclear powers.

3. The Soviet Union is clearly interested in preserving a stable strategic relationship with the United States. It strongly resists the further spread of nuclear weapons, preferring a nuclear world which is more manageable and uncomplicated by the emergence of new nuclear powers. A sharp increase in the strategic nuclear capabilities of the superpowers could possibly motivate some of the threshold nuclear powers to abandon their self-restraint and to seek security in indigenous or shared nuclear capabilities.

4. Current and foreseeable Soviet security and policy interests depend on stable strategic deterrence and flexible uses of their conventional capabilities. A stabilization of Soviet-American strategic capabilities at approximate parity levels would still give the Soviet Union a wide range of options for the pursuit of policy objectives by means of conventional forces.

Thus, various Soviet analysts currently argue that "traditional concepts of power do not fit in this age,"[45] or stress that "those who relied on the atomic bomb as a guarantee of their security found themselves less and less secure as the years passed by."[46] And though Soviet writers usually ascribe this change in attitude to the United States, they undoubtedly recognize that it also fully applies to the Soviet Union: "U.S. military power is always increasing while its political weight is always decreasing in the world. The evidence is the

[45] V. Glazunov, Radio Moscow, June 28, 1968.

[46] M. Maratov, "Ways of Solving the Atom Problem," *International Affairs* (Moscow), August 1966, p. 9.

inability of the United States, which is militarily strong, to crush the will of a small country. This may seem at a first glance to be inconsistent; in fact it is not."[47]

In arguing the diminished political and military utility of vast strategic power, the Soviets also stress the community of superpower concerns and interests, the major responsibility of the superpowers for international stability. This attitude reflects traditional Soviet "realism" and a desire to keep the management of central international issues uncomplicated. In matters of arms control, the Soviet Union has shown a clear preference for Soviet-American initiatives which would, at least initially, exclude other countries.

Resistance from smaller states to this specter of superpower condominium has been evident in the Third World, in the West, and in communist areas, too. A Yugoslav political analyst recently wrote that "the two biggest powers have long since oriented themselves toward avoiding a major thermonuclear war . . . [and] toward preservation of their monopoly position as regards solution of the principal problems of the world." He added that "this course has worked to the advantage of the superpowers as their influence over world affairs has been and still is on the rise."[48] The Yugoslav Assistant Secretary of Foreign Affairs Belovskii noted that "most of the conflicts convulsing the world derive from the inability of great and powerful countries to grasp the indispensability" of a more active participation of smaller countries in international

[47] Radio Moscow, June 28, 1968.
[48] Dr. Brezaric, "Relations Between Washington and Moscow," *Review of International Affairs* (Belgrade), no. 449 (December 20, 1968), p. 9.

affairs.[49] A Rumanian political leader, in a pointed though oblique stab at the Soviet Union, asked if it is "admissible that almost all states of the world—in general the small and medium states—should be subjected to control, and [that] . . . the nuclear powers should dodge every measure of controls."[50]

The Soviets reject such accusations and demands for greater participation by small and medium states, dismissing them as "demagogic theses about the 'haves' and 'have-nots'" and as "notions that the nuclear powers have allegedly 'made better provisions for themselves' to guarantee their security and other 'blessings.'"[51] While piously maintaining that "nuclear disarmament requires the participation of all nuclear states," the Soviets are quick to assert that "at the same time the correlation of strategic forces on an international scale is now such that the efforts of the United States and the Soviet Union—which possess the greatest nuclear potential—aimed at the liquidation of the strategic arms race could greatly promote the security interests of other countries too. . . ."[52]

The Soviets thus prefer to retain strategic bipolarity in a multipolar political world. Among the programmatic objectives for this Soviet position are the formal establishment of full political and strategic Soviet superpower equality with the United States, and

[49] D. Belovskii, "Security Through Disarmament," *Review of International Affairs* (Belgrade), no. 444 (October 5, 1968), p. 4.

[50] N. Ecobesco, *Agerpress* (Bucharest), February 6, 1968.

[51] S. Beglov, *Izvestiia*, September 26, 1968.

[52] "Observer," *Pravda*, March 7, 1970. This article is generally assumed in the West to reflect the official position of the Soviet Politburo, and thus represents the most current and authoritative statement of the Soviet position toward SALT.

the desire to keep arms control issues separate from other international problems. Indeed, one sore point in past Soviet attitudes toward the United States was the assumed U.S. unwillingness to consider the Soviets as political and strategic equals. Khrushchev repeatedly raised this issue, maintaining that "President Kennedy once admitted that our strength is equal . . . and it is high time that . . . American leaders should come to correct conclusions and pursue a reasonable policy." He plaintively asked "how then does the admission of our equal military capabilities tally with such unequal relations between our great states?"[53] Even the current leadership found it troublesome that despite assumed equality of American and Soviet forces "some generals and even responsible US state leaders fly into passion and thoughtlessly and rashly maintain the opposite."[54] The Soviets continue to reject "the illusionary quality of the calculations of those who have tried to talk to the Soviet Union 'from a position of strength.' . . . No one can have, nor must have any illusions on this score."[55]

The second Soviet objective, to keep arms control talks separate from other outstanding issues, needs somewhat broader examination. It has been suggested above that a confluence of certain political, strategic, and psychological conditions has created a conducive climate and motivation for Soviet consideration of arms control talks. It has also been suggested that Soviet arms control overtures seem realistic and credible. However, it appears that such Soviet interests in stra-

[53] *Pravda*, October 28, 1962.
[54] Party General Secretary Brezhnev, *Pravda*, July 2, 1966.
[55] "Observer."

tegic arms limitation talks with the United States are not an end in themselves, but rather serve several broader objectives. In a sense, we may describe this broad Soviet policy line, of which SALT is a very important aspect, as a hold-and-explore policy, something in the nature of an emerging grand design for the 1970s.

This postulated hold-and-explore policy derives from changing Soviet policy interests, emerging new commitments, and from some policy initiatives recently undertaken by the Soviets. The assumed objectives of such a policy would be to *hold* onto and stabilize the western flank of the Soviet Union (NATO, the United States, and Eastern Europe), while gaining greater freedom to deal with the mounting challenge of Communist China, and to *explore* policy opportunities in the "soft" and presumably less contested areas south of Russia (the Middle East, the Mediterranean, and North Africa). Such a policy line would shift the center of gravity of Soviet strategic and political activity from a predominantly western orientation to a southern and eastern one. This presumably would be a policy with relatively low costs, low risks, and potentially high payoffs for the Soviets, while a continued pursuit of former policies would appear to be high in costs and risks and low in payoffs.

Recent Soviet diplomatic, political, and military activities suggest the emergence of such a policy orientation. The Soviets have shown strong interest in SALT and in stabilizing European security arrangements. At the same time, they have been strengthening their forces in the Far East along the Sino-Soviet borders while retaining and expanding their position in the

Middle East and the Mediterranean region. While Soviet-American interests converge on issues of SALT, Soviet interests in the various regions of the world are quite different from those of the United States. Thus, the Soviets prefer to keep SALT apart from other outstanding international problems.

## Technical Considerations

In considering Soviet motivations, incentives, and disincentives regarding arms control, one must sooner or later connect such problems to matters of strategic balance and to perceptions about the consequences of various strategic ratios between the two superpowers.

In a recent, widely noted article, McGeorge Bundy advanced several challenging propositions. He maintained that "the neglected truth about the present strategic arms race between the United States and the Soviet Union is that in terms of international political behavior that race has now become almost completely irrelevant" since the new weapons developed by the two powers "will provide neither protection nor opportunity in any serious political sense." "[T]he internal politics of the strategic arms race has remained the prisoner of its technology."[56] In a sense, Bundy reiterated some of the thoughts of former Secretary of Defense McNamara, who in 1967 stated that the concept of "superiority" or "first strike" had little significance in contemporary circumstances since both sides have built up their second-strike capabilities "to the point that a first strike capability on either side has become

[56] McGeorge Bundy, "To Cap the Volcano," *Foreign Affairs*, no. 1 (October 1969).

unattainable." And thus, the reality of a Soviet first-strike threat had become essentially "irrelevant" since the Soviet Union could "effectively destroy the United States even after absorbing the full weight of the American first strike."[57] The Soviets have been saying similar things in recent years, strongly rejecting the concept of strategic superiority, maintaining that "with every passing year the arms race becomes increasingly more unpromising" and "judging from everything, a new spiral in the arms race could not change the essence"[58] of the current military balance between the two powers.

We ought to consider in our analysis, however, the prevailing strategic calculus which informs formal Soviet and American strategic and arms control policy. Even if we could agree with Mr. Bundy's assertion that "think-tank analysts" live in "an unreal world" because "they can assume that the loss of dozens of great cities is somehow a real choice for sane men,"[59] we must still examine the technological-strategic considerations relevant to current arms control policies.

Strategic arms limitation offers the first major test for the two superpowers in circumstances which may be described as a nonzero sum situation, i.e., both adversaries must clearly gain from such arrangements, while making sure that their vital security and political interests remain intact. There are at least three factors to be considered in this connection: the evolving strategic-technological balance and perceptions of its implications for the security and policy interests of the two countries; the timing element, which is pre-

[57] Robert McNamara, speech given in San Francisco, September 18, 1967.

[58] "Observer."

[59] Bundy, "To Cap the Volcano."

sumably important to arms control negotiations; and the perceptions of the adversaries regarding their respective capabilities and intentions.

It is widely assumed both in the West and in the Soviet Union that "a unique point in history has been reached. An indisputable state of strategic nuclear parity exists between the two superpowers." Moreover, "if this is the moment for arms control, then it remains to be seized" because "in the interim, the momentum of technology and deployment goes on, moving us to a point where—in the absence of substantive talks or agreements—totally new responses to these deployments will be politically justifiable in this country, and the arms race will have blown its best opportunity to cool off."[60] The author, writing in November 1969, added that the point of no return would likely be one year away.

The urgent stress on the propitious timing for arms control agreements was described by the Soviets as "one of those rare moments in history . . . when both sides are ready to admit equality in the broadest sense and to view this as an initial position for reaching agreement concerning the freezing and the subsequent reduction of arms." They also urged the politicians "not to let the chance slip away."[61]

What these authors, and many others, were describing was an unprecedented strategic relationship between the superpowers, that of strategic equality. They also warned that this brief pause in the action-reaction dynamics would not last long since new and profoundly disturbing weapons were already being tested,

[60] Michael Getler, "Arms Control and the SS-9," *Space-Aeronautics*, November 1969, p. 40.
[61] *Pravda*, July 7, 1968.

and eventual deployment would enormously complicate the possibilities for real arms control. These weapons systems include MIRVs and the contemplated expansion of ABM systems.

The strategic capabilities of the Soviet Union and the United States, before the new weapons systems were designed, satisfied several basic security requirements. Each possessed a credible, nearly invulnerable, retaliatory second strike capability, thus creating stable deterrence. Such systems made surprise or first-strike attacks suicidal, since the aggressor was almost certain to receive the full brunt of a retaliatory second strike. For purposes of arms control, such a system had further advantages. Modern reconnaissance technology was able to verify the adversary's strategic capabilities with a great degree of accuracy, thus offering assurance against any surprise. Reconnaissance could also provide credible assessments of adversary testing techniques, deployment programs, and the like. This is an important consideration since the Soviets (and to a large extent the United States) strongly oppose on-site inspection proposals as part of potential arms control agreements. In sum, the deterrence system was quite stable; the element of uncertainty was tolerable; there were low incentives for considering first-strike attacks; and arms control was theoretically feasible.

Developments of the late 1960s and early 1970s, however, have progressively eroded the propitiousness of arms control talks.[62] The Soviet Union has continued to deploy the SS-9 missile and the United States

[62] Recent statistics on U.S. and U.S.S.R. arms programs are not reassuring about the prospects for arms control. Before the MIRV technology and strategy appeared, the Soviet Union and the United States possessed relatively balanced capabilities. The

has continued to test its new MIRV systems. The SS-9 is a very powerful missile which can accommodate a large single payload or a sizable number (up to fifteen) of smaller individual warheads. The American MIRV system is roughly similar in that its Poseidon and Minuteman III missiles can be fitted with multiple, independently targeted warheads. The basic problem with these weapons is that they are highly destabilizing. They can be considered as a first-strike, counterforce weapon intended to destroy the adversary's retaliatory force.[63] They can, in principle, saturate the

---

United States had about 2,500 warheads distributed over 1,000 ICBMs (Minuteman), 656 Polaris SLBMs, some 50 Titan IIs, and others. The Soviets have about 1,700 warheads distributed over some 300 SS-9s, about 1,000 SS-11 and SS-13 missiles, and some 300 SLBMs. It is estimated that by 1976 MIRV capabilities for the United States will amount to about 10,000 warheads (in Polaris-based Poseidon missiles and land-based Minuteman missiles). It is estimated that the navy's MIRV program alone will cost about $18 billion by 1975. Moreover, the Defense Department is already contemplating newer weapons systems with such acronyms as ABRES, ULMS, SABMIS, SAM-D, and others. Some of these weapons systems will have "smart" warheads (capable of taking evasive action) as opposed to current "dumb" warheads. See Ralph E. Lapp, "Can SALT Stop MIRV?" *New York Times Magazine*, February 1, 1970.

[63] M. Getler, in his authoritative analysis observes that the SS-9 is "the most destabilizing" of the new weapons, representing "one of the major perturbations in strategic weaponry since the nuclear age began." The Soviets, on the other hand, point at official U.S. descriptions of MIRV weapons, which to them clearly suggest their first-strike intent and capability. A January 1968 Defense Department statement on MIRVs maintained that "they will be far better suited for the destruction of hardened enemy sites than any existing missile warheads." Secretary Laird, on April 1, 1969, said that an improved accuracy of Poseidon missiles would "enhance its effectiveness against hard targets." *New York Times*, February 1, 1970.

defenses of the opponent and thus render him even more vulnerable. Finally, they cannot be detected in the usual manner, and thus they introduce a strong new element of uncertainty, which reinforces the "worst plausible case" approach to defense and politics.

The role of the ABM in the context of MIRV and SS-9 is ambiguous. In the prevailing strategic parlance, the argument against a "thick" ABM system is that it is both very expensive and militarily futile since the enemy would presumably saturate the defenses with massive salvos of warheads, and at the same time it is unnecessarily provocative, motivating the adversary to strengthen his efforts to make sure he can annihilate such defenses, thus adding further to the arms race. Both sides are currently proceeding with extensive testing of the MIRV and SS-9 systems, and it is not very likely that these programs will be halted or reversed.

Though it is not unlikely that the Soviet-American arms control talks in Vienna or any future talks elsewhere may bring about some substantial agreement to prevent the deployment of the new strategic weapons, we must still contemplate President Nixon's recent statement that "the more intense the [arms] competition the greater the uncertainty about the other side's intentions."[64] And all available information suggests that both the Soviet Union and the United States are engaged in an intense arms competition, considering construction, testing, or deployment of various arms systems, both of the "old" variety and of the new

[64] A report to the Congress by Richard Nixon, President of the United States, *U.S. Foreign Policy for the 1970s; A New Strategy for Peace*, February 18, 1970, p. 142.

ones.[65] And parallel to this development, there is mounting uncertainty on both sides about the intentions and objectives that underlie it.

An interesting Soviet argument echoes that of McGeorge Bundy, namely, that in the United States technological considerations frequently determine major political or strategic problems. To the Soviets, accustomed to the intensely political environment of their decision-making, this presumed phenomenon is highly disturbing since "policy may itself become the captive of the scientific elite." From the Soviet point of view, "the technical approach to the problem of national security led to serious changes in the strategic, military and—what is especially dangerous—in the political thinking in the United States. . . . With this approach the question of war itself appears to be divorced from policy and from the analysis of whether war would or would not achieve the desired political goals."[66] Thus, the Soviets believe the technological elite is responsible for propelling the momentum of warfare technology to ever higher levels.

Soviet suspicions concerning U.S. intentions in SALT focus also on the U.S. military establishment. Thus "the defense secretary [Laird] is lavishly spicing his demands for the intensification of the arms race with references to the mythical 'Soviet Threat,' " and consequently "it is impossible not to be alarmed by how often and how many times the defense secretary dis-

[65] See "A Statement by Secretary of Defense Melvin R. Laird," *Defense Program and Budget, Fiscal Year 1971*, February 20, 1970, *passim*.

[66] "Between Helsinki and Vienna," *USA: Economics, Politics, Ideology* (Moscow), January 1970, pp. 60–64.

cusses Pentagon plans for creating new offensive strategic weapons." The Soviets maintain, therefore, that there are powerful forces in the West "that are not too pleased with the talks on the restriction of strategic weapons and even less pleased with the prospect of an agreement between the USSR and the United States on this question."[67]

What troubles Soviet diplomatic and military elements is the question "to what extent do Secretary Laird's militaristic appeals reflect the position of the U.S. Government?"[68] More specifically, they allude to recent statements from the Defense Department regarding the uses and objectives of the MIRV weapons. Statements by Secretary Laird and Dr. John Foster suggest to the Soviets that MIRV is intended as a first-strike weapon against the Soviet Union, which presumably contradicts official U.S. policy.

If the Soviets are having trouble assessing the U.S. strategic and political intent in connection with SALT, the American side is not much better off. The Soviets now urge that "a serious and honest approach be taken by both sides, an approach shorn of intention to achieve unilateral advantages by means of talks, or to utilize the talks as a cover for the development of a new round in the arms race."[69] Yet in talking with various Soviet diplomats and military people, and in reading through the Soviet press, one encounters evidence of a muffled, but nevertheless real, sense of disagreement within the Soviet bureaucratic elite regarding the utility, timeliness, and viability of SALT.

[67] "Observer."
[68] *Ibid.*
[69] *Ibid.*

Typical of such militant and certainly bellicose Soviet views is an article contained in *Red Star*, the military's main organ.[70] The author warns his audience of the need to order economic and social priorities in the state in the interests of the defense establishment. He evokes various Leninist dicta to impress upon the party leadership the fact that a policy that does not try to "prepare itself to master all types of weapons and means of warfare which the enemy has, or might have, is senseless and even criminal." He concludes on the somber note that all measures must be undertaken for "the attainment of superiority over the enemy in the balance of forces." One wonders whether such statements represent official Soviet policy.

Contemplation of arms control arrangements between the superpowers unleashes renewed fears, mistrust, and expectations of threat. It is not the most desirable milieu in which to seek agreements intended to halt and reverse the powerful forces which have dominated our lives in the past two decades.

## Summary

Certain basic changes have occurred in recent years in international affairs that have brought about reappraisals and new attitudes in the Kremlin. First, modern warfare technology has introduced a momentum in the nuclear arms race without commensurate political gains. Second, having finally caught up with the United States in strategic weapons systems, the

[70] Major General, Doctor of Military Sciences A. Lagovskii, "The Economy and the Military Might of the State," *Krasnaia zvezda*, September 25, 1969.

Soviet Union has obtained a dearly sought objective. Third, this balance of terror acts as a central regulatory mechanism in international relations, and the Soviet Union strongly desires to maintain the stability of this deterrence relationship. Fourth, this desired stability is being increasingly threatened by destabilizing pressures of proliferation, nationalism, and, most importantly, a new cycle in the arms race.

Arms control would thus seem attractive to Soviet leaders. Ratification of the Nonproliferation Treaty is likely to affirm a desirable superpower nuclear hegemony and hinder the emergence of troublesome political actors with nuclear capabilities. An agreement on nonexpansion of ABM capabilities beyond the "thin" levels would also serve Soviet defense interests. An agreement not to deploy MIRVs would prevent an escalation of U.S. offensive capabilities and, in turn, that of the Soviet Union, and it would preclude the need for inspection beyond the currently used orbital verification systems. A successful arms limitation agreement with the United States would free the Soviet Union from the need to keep up with the more productive and vastly more capable U.S. defense industries. At the same time, such an arrangement would not endanger Soviet security interests and would indeed free the leadership to pursue national objectives in a less constrained manner. In other words, for the Soviet Union, arms control would seem to be a variant of its strategic policy—it would achieve cheaply and adequately what a protracted and expensive arms race would presumably achieve.

A workable arms control arrangement, however, must clear formidable hurdles before it can ever become a reality. The problem of verification and inspection alone seems at present to defy solution. Soviet insistence on national sovereignty and on denying international verification must be overcome before any fruitful talks can be concluded. The problem of the negotiations process itself, whereby protracted negotiations would take place while testing and deployment of planned or ongoing weapons systems would continue, must be tackled at the outset, or it could preclude the achievement of the intended objectives. The definition of "nonstrategic" forces could become troublesome unless a clear understanding of their type and purpose is reached at the outset.

Soviet leaders have in the past used disarmament overtures and peace campaigns as tactical devices to divide or confuse their adversaries, or to gain time. They also have a strong predilection for large, unfettered indigenous forces, and disarmament is "unnatural" to them. Nevertheless, though the Soviets' declaratory policy is an uncertain guide, and though their real motives are somewhat obscure, the United States would still be well advised to take recent Soviet proposals for arms control seriously. The Soviet Union has in recent years made great strides in terms of its national security, economic strength, and political influence. The present Soviet leaders would be likely to make significant accommodations to safeguard these achievements, which would be threatened in a world of nuclear anarchy, eroding deterrents, and a renewed arms race.

Whether reasonable and workable arms control arrangements are made will depend on many factors. Key among them will be a reciprocal understanding regarding common needs—mutually acceptable objectives that transcend mutual trust. A workable arms control arrangement is, in essence, a formalization of certain rules of behavior among states. It also serves as a way of communicating intentions regarding the uses of economic and technological resources for political and military objectives.

It is important to consider the history of Soviet technological and military development. The Soviets have over the past two decades sought systematically and with considerable success to overcome deficiencies in their strategic technologies. They ended the U.S. atomic bomb monopoly several years earlier than most western experts expected; thermonuclear weapons were developed almost simultaneously in both countries; and the Soviet Union was the first to test an ICBM successfully in flight. While the Soviet Union lagged behind the United States in the procurement of ICBM systems, this was the result more of political calculations than of an inability to do so. This gap has been closed in recent years, and the Soviet Union has come close to equalling U.S. strategic capabilities. It would be imprudent, therefore, to assume that the Soviet Union is not capable of making great and rapid strides in the development and deployment of military technologies, if circumstances should demand it. We must not forget the rather sanguine assessments in 1965 of very knowledgeable American leaders that the Soviet leaders "have decided that they have lost the quantitative race, and they are not seeking to engage us in that contest. . . . There is no indication that the Soviets are seeking to develop a strategic nuclear force as large as ours."[71] Current U.S. assessments of Soviet strategic capabilities offer a rather melancholy negation of those projections. Thus, since the Soviet Union seems serious about realistic arms limitations talks, and since such talks and arrangements would also serve U.S. interests, further talks on substantive issues should be pursued. At the same time, we should remain alert to the fact that strategic arms limitation is not an end in itself to Soviet leaders, but rather a key objective in their new policy direction: to stabilize an expensive and counterproductive arms race at desirable levels, while gaining greater freedom to pursue policy opportunities in other areas.

[71] Robert S. McNamara, in *U.S. News and World Report*, April 12, 1965, p. 52.

# 3

## Nuclear Proliferation and
## Soviet Arms Control Policy

IN SHARP CONTRAST TO Moscow's lack of interest until recently in strategic arms limitation negotiations, concern over the threat of nuclear dispersion has been a consistent theme in Soviet disarmament policy for well over a decade. The main origins of this concern date back to the Allied Powers' decision in 1955 to allow the rearming of West Germany; since then, the fear has become ingrained in the Soviet Union that its former adversary might somehow gain possession of nuclear weapons. More recently, Soviet disquiet over the proliferation specter has taken on added intensity because of the ominous implications posed by Communist China's incipient nuclear capability. And the fact that nuclear weapons will soon be within the easy technological grasp of many smaller countries has lately imparted a new immediacy to Moscow's nonproliferation efforts.

Particularly during the past several years, Soviet pronouncements on the proliferation issue have frequently bordered on the apocalyptic. One prominent Soviet analyst described nuclear proliferation as "one of the most burning problems of our day."[1] Another commentator, contemplating the image of a world ridden with nuclear *nouveaux riches*, each crowding both the superpowers and one another for a measure of international stature and influence, likened such a situation to "a gigantic powder keg ready to explode with the tiniest spark."[2] The urgency reflected in these statements, moreover, has been matched by an energetic Soviet policy commitment to nonproliferation which has borne all the earmarks of a concerted diplomatic crusade.[3] The Soviet leaders' persistent efforts to get the Nuclear Nonproliferation Treaty (NPT) accepted and implemented, their eager endorsement of the Nuclear Test Ban Treaty in 1963, their implacable opposition to various NATO nuclear-sharing arrangements like the abortive multilateral nuclear force, and their

[1] G. Gerasimov, "Accidental War," *International Affairs* (Moscow), no. 12 (December 1966), p. 38.

[2] Editorial, "For the Good of All People," *Izvestiia*, June 21, 1968.

[3] In this respect, Moscow's handling of the proliferation problem has not differed substantially from that of the United States. Indeed, it should be made clear that none of the points developed in this chapter are intended to suggest that the Soviet Union's reactions to the proliferation problem have been in any sense unique. Much of what is said here about Soviet policy is easily applicable to the United States as well. One of the better examples of "official" U.S. thinking on the proliferation issue is William C. Foster, "New Directions in Arms Control and Disarmament," *Foreign Affairs*, vol. 43, no. 4 (July 1965), pp. 587–601. For a thoughtful and provocative critique of that position, see also William B. Bader, *The United States and the Spread of Nuclear Weapons* (New York: Pegasus, 1968).

continued diplomatic pursuit of regional nuclear free zones throughout the world all testify to their special interest in preventing the spread of nuclear weaponry.

How are we to explain this concern in terms of the Soviet hierarchy of disarmament interests? Have they sought merely to preserve the existing Soviet-American nuclear duopoly as a permanent feature of the international landscape?[4] Or are they genuinely concerned about the real dangers and instabilities which a multi-nuclear world might introduce? Have Soviet statements asserting the general undesirability of proliferation simply been aimed at cloaking Moscow's parochial opposition to West German nuclear accession behind a façade of righteous concern for international security?[5] Or can we really sense a feeling of genuine Soviet trepidation over the larger "Nth-country" problem as well? If the latter is the case, then how do the Soviets

[4] Raymond Aron, for example, has described the Soviet-American opposition to proliferation as a reflection of their supposed common interest in "the perpetuation of the thermonuclear duopoly (or quasi-duopoly)." *The Great Debate: Theories of Nuclear Strategy* (New York: Doubleday and Company, 1965), pp. 230–31.

[5] One West German writer, Gerhard Wettig, maintains that Moscow's expressed concerns over the "Nth-country" nuclear threat have merely been a front to cover the primary Soviet interest in forestalling the development of a German nuclear capability. See his "Funktionen eines Sperrvertrages in der sowjetischen Politik" (The Role of the Nonproliferation Treaty in Soviet Policy), *Aussenpolitik*, no. 1 (January 1968), p. 10. Similarly, Thomas W. Wolfe has noted the "importance which the Soviet Union attaches to employing a . . . nonproliferation treaty as a means of blocking German access to nuclear weapons." *The Soviet Union and Arms Control* (P-3337; Santa Monica, Cal.: The RAND Corporation, April 1966), p. 13.

perceive the likely prospects and consequences of nuclear diffusion to various areas of the world? Are all forms
of proliferation equally reprehensible to the Soviets,
as many of their public statements would have us believe, or do they in reality accept a more pragmatic
view of the problem which distinguishes varying levels
of proliferation threat and tolerability? And finally,
how does the proliferation issue relate to the larger
Soviet interest in strategic arms limitation talks with
the United States, and what effect might it have on
the prospects for success in those talks? It is these
questions to which this chapter is primarily addressed.[6]

## SOVIET PERSPECTIVES ON NUCLEAR DIFFUSION

Many Soviet statements on the proliferation issue
contend that any further nuclear spread—whatever its
form and wherever its locus—would both seriously
endanger international security and substantially
undermine the chances for a fruitful Soviet-American
strategic arms limitation dialogue. The magnitude of
this proliferation threat was adumbrated in the following scenario advanced by *Pravda*'s Yuri Zhukov. "The
danger of proliferation of nuclear arms is becoming
more real every day. . . . At least ten countries in

---

[6] Since the major focus of this chapter is on the policy implications of the proliferation issue, no attempt has been made to
reconstruct the various diplomatic "mechanics" which guided past
Soviet-American negotiatory maneuvering over the Nonproliferation Treaty itself. An overview of the history of Soviet-American
nonproliferation negotiations, however, may be found in Walter
C. Clemens, Jr., *The Arms Race and Sino-Soviet Relations*
(Stanford, Cal.: The Hoover Institution on War, Revolution,
and Peace, 1968), pp. 120–71.

addition to the existing nuclear powers have, or soon will have, the capability for producing nuclear bombs. Between this year and 1970 these ten countries, should they so desire, could produce 1000 bombs per year."[7]

The suggestion that a resolution of the proliferation problem would be a necessary precondition for any further arms control advances was given· particular emphasis by *Izvestiia*'s authoritative political commentator, Vikenty Matveyev, precisely at the time the Soviet Union first broached its interest in discussing a strategic weapons limitation agreement with the United States. "Looking to the future, we must not be distracted from the task that is more urgent now. This is to ensure the broadest support by the governments of all continents for the nuclear nonproliferation treaty. *Progress in the field of disarmament will depend above all on this.*"[8]

These two themes, each of which has been a central component in Soviet arguments supporting the Nonproliferation Treaty, reflect a number of underlying premises and assumptions. The notion that nuclear acquisition by any presently nonnuclear country would invariably spark a contagious spread of atomic weaponry, for example, has periodically been discussed even by members of the Soviet political elite. In 1964, party ideologist Suslov alluded to this supposedly "virulent"

[7] "A Pressing Problem," *Pravda*, May 26, 1968.

[8] "Let Us Advance Further," *Izvestiia*, July 3, 1968 (emphasis added). Matveyev elsewhere pointed out, in a similar vein, that "if nuclear weapons started to spread all over the world it would hardly be possible to talk seriously and realistically about the problem of disarmament." Radio Moscow, Domestic Service, June 30, 1968.

potential of nuclear spread as having been a major factor behind Moscow's decision to terminate nuclear weapons assistance to Communist China:

> The CPSU Central Committee and the Soviet Government have already explained why we do not believe it expedient to help China in the production of nuclear weapons. It would inevitably arouse in return a reaction in the nuclear arming of the states of the imperialist camp, including West Germany and Japan. These countries, being better developed economically and scientifically, could certainly have produced more bombs than China and could have created a nuclear potential with greater speed.[9]

More recently, this same position was stated categorically by *Pravda*'s Fyodor Burlatskii on the eve of the Soviet Union's signing of the NPT. "The acquisition of nuclear weapons [by a state]," he observed, "would inevitably give rise to a chain reaction. The friends and foes of the country in question would also seek those weapons."[10] Similar assertions have been voiced

[9] *Pravda*, April 3, 1964. The Soviet Union has, in fact, been far from blameless in the matter of Peking's current nuclear weapons development. During the late 1950s, precisely at the time it was beginning its diplomatic advocacy of nonproliferation, Moscow was engaged in a program of nuclear weapons technical assistance to Peking. One may, of course, argue that this assistance program was inspired by the Soviet Union's desire to retain as much control as possible over what would most likely have become, sooner or later, an indigenous Chinese nuclear program in any event. The fact remains, nonetheless, that the Soviet Union today has largely itself to thank for the problems it now confronts as a result of Communist China's accession to nuclear power status.

[10] F. Burlatskii, "Problems Affecting All Mankind," *Pravda*, February 15, 1967.

by other Soviet spokesmen over the past several years,[11] all variations on the theme that nuclear diffusion would spread like wildfire if allowed to get started, that it is therefore essential that effective blocks be placed in its path while there is still time, and that the solution lies in general international acceptance of the Non-proliferation Treaty.

Soviet statements opposing nuclear spread have also frequently implied that proliferation is not, by and large, reducible into individual categories of relative "acceptability." These statements, admittedly, have been devoid of any explicit pronouncements along this line. But the inclination to treat the proliferation challenge simply as a generic "Nth-power" problem suggests a Soviet reluctance to consider possible variants of nuclear diffusion, inspired by different local conditions with various degrees of threat potential to the super-powers, disruptive potential in the international arena, and propensity to invite proliferation elsewhere. This tendency to "universalize" the proliferation challenge was evident in an official statement issued in 1963, again aimed at explaining Moscow's reasons for terminating its nuclear weapons assistance to the Chinese. "It would be naïve, to say the least, to assume that it is possible to conduct one policy in the West and another in the East, to fight with one hand against the arming of West Germany with nuclear weapons,

[11] Igor Orlov, for example, remarked that if new states acquired nuclear weapons, "we could of course expect a rapid proliferation of nuclear weapons, a chain reaction exceedingly undesirable for all . . . [which] would be followed by a considerable mounting of the nuclear menace." TASS International Service, May 20, 1968.

against the spreading of nuclear weapons in the world, and to supply these weapons to China on the other hand."[12]

Perhaps the central objection which the Soviets have raised against nuclear spread, however, stems from their asserted belief that any expansion of the "nuclear club" beyond its present dimensions "would greatly aggravate international tensions and increase the possibility of these monstrous mass destruction weapons being brought into play."[13] To support such pronouncements, the Soviets have advanced several lines of reasoning. Perhaps the most frequent one has been their suggestion that, at the very least, the widespread availability of atomic weapons would significantly increase the mere statistical probability that those weapons would eventually be used—either by

[12] Soviet government statement to the CPR, August 21, 1963, cited in Harold C. Hinton, *Communist China in World Politics* (Boston: Houghton Mifflin Company, 1966), p. 474. One can argue, to be sure, that the "real" reasons behind Moscow's nuclear aid refusal to China were informed rather substantially more by hardheaded strategic pragmatism than by considerations of diplomatic imagery. Yet during that same period, U.S. proposals for a NATO multilateral nuclear force were being bombarded with vitriolic Soviet attacks charging, in effect, that by providing West Germany with access to the nuclear trigger, while at the same time mouthing pious platitudes in Geneva regarding nonproliferation, the West was trying to have the best of two worlds. To the extent, therefore, that Moscow felt compelled to emphasize the incompatibility between the spirit of nonproliferation and the reality of western nuclear-sharing proposals, the Soviets could scarcely avoid applying the same principle to themselves in regard to Communist China.

[13] "An Important Aspect of Disarmament," *International Affairs* (Moscow), no. 1 (January 1967), p. 67.

accident, by miscalculation, or through some sort of "irrational" impulse—with all sorts of untold risks and consequences. One Soviet civilian writer on strategic affairs, G. Gerasimov, pointed out the "link between the problem of accidental war and the question of which country will next acquire nuclear weapons," and noted that "without discussing the matter in detail, one may merely say that the proliferation of nuclear weapons increases the chances of accident." Moreover, he went on to warn, "the fact that no such accident has yet occurred is no guarantee that it will not."[14] Another spokesman emphasized the heightened "risk of both technical and political mistakes" which presumably would exist in a world pervaded with nuclear powers. "Have there ever been any occasions," he asked, "when generals have refused to use an effective weapon? And is it not possible that some irresponsible persons might give the order for the use of weapons of mass destruction?"[15]

A different approach which the Soviets have taken in discussing the destabilizing potential of nuclear spread has been to point out the possibility that a catalytic war could drag the two superpowers inexorably into a nuclear confrontation against both their will and their interests. Yuri Zhukov, for example, reflected in *Pravda* that "if the atomic bomb exploded anywhere, it would be very difficult to halt the spread of a war which utilized mass means of destruction."[16]

[14] "Accidental War," *International Affairs* (Moscow), no. 12 (December 1966), p. 38.

[15] Viktor Shragin, Radio Moscow, Domestic Service, March 19, 1967.

[16] "A Pressing Problem," *Pravda*, May 26, 1968.

Another Soviet article alluded to the problem of catalytic war in this self-serving, but nonetheless revealing, reference to the German problem: "The United States is forced to accept an agreement on nonproliferation in view of the sharpening interimperialist contradictions. It fears that nuclear weapons may fall into the hands of its partners, who could involve them in a nuclear war independently of the intentions of the US ruling circles themselves."[17]

In general, assertions of these sorts have sought to underscore the disruptive potential which nuclear dispersion would introduce into the international system; to emphasize the "worst possible cases" which could possibly result from that disruptiveness; and consequently, to bolster the argument for nuclear nonproliferation as an imperative precondition for a stable international balance of power.

A final Soviet argument is that if nuclear spread is not decisively prevented in its incipient stage, it will rapidly acquire such momentum as to become virtually unmanageable either by the "enlightened paternalism" of the two superpowers or by any self-equilibrating mechanisms which may regulate the international system as a whole. Most Soviet statements to this effect have not ventured to justify the proposition through any detailed or systematic analysis, but rather have merely held it out as an article of faith, as a

[17] N. Nikolayev and V. Shestov, "Decisive Round at Geneva," *International Affairs* (Moscow), no. 3 (March 1968), p. 7. Interestingly, one need only substitute here "Kremlin decision-makers" for "U.S. ruling circles" and "Sino-Soviet conflict" for "interimperialist contradictions" to see the reflection of this problem in the Soviet mirror.

sort of resigned recognition of some internal determinism which will inevitably drive the process of nuclear spread to its natural, apocalyptic conclusion. This concern with the irreversibility of proliferation was voiced by an *Izvestiia* political observer, Viktor Shragin, in a Radio Moscow round-table discussion several months prior to the NPT signing:

> What will happen if new nuclear arsenals start to germinate from existing ones, and if other states set about creating their own nuclear weapons or gaining access to them? The answer is obvious: it will be virtually impossible any longer to stop the process of the spread of nuclear weapons throughout the world. Nuclear rivalry will become even more acute. The risk of war with the use of mass-destruction weapons will have increased many times over. Such is the real danger threatening the world.[18]

Such arguments underscore what Moscow has maintained to be the profound urgency of getting general international agreement on nonproliferation while there is still some time left, and to emphasize its belief that such agreement will have to come before any other arms control measures that might be on the agenda can be addressed. A statement issued in May 1968 by TASS summed it up this way: "Failure to solve this task will, no doubt, arrest and complicate the solution of other disarmament problems for a long time."[19]

The general tenor of these statements would, by itself, suggest that Moscow has regarded the threat of nuclear spread as a matter of the most prepossessing

[18] Viktor Shragin, Radio Moscow, March 19, 1967.
[19] Igor Orlov, TASS International Service, May 20, 1968.

alarm and foreboding. Yet paradoxically enough, there remains the glaring fact that five nations already possess atomic weapons, with no currently visible signs either that a chain reaction of nuclear proliferation is about to occur or that the international balance of power is in any imminent danger of being upset. On the contrary, the emergence of an acknowledged mutual deterrence system between the two superpowers and the clear dominance of this system over the rather symbolic nuclear capabilities of the other three atomic powers seem, if anything, to have heightened rather than diminished the stability of the international system at the strategic nuclear level. Why, then, should the Soviets have shown such disquiet over the possibility of a sixth (or even a seventh) power acquiring nuclear weapons? For if such a development would indeed produce the dire consequences which Soviet statements have enumerated, then why have those consequences not yet become manifest in what today is already a multinuclear world? Why, in other words, should the emergence of one more nuclear-armed state provoke a chain of events which the existence of five such states has somehow managed to avoid?

The answer, it seems, is that the real nature of the proliferation problem is rather different from that portrayed in Soviet disarmament pronouncements. The fact that possession of nuclear arms by five countries has neither sparked a mad rush by other states for similar weapons nor significantly altered the traditional pattern of superpower dominance in international politics raises basic questions about the validity of two central propositions in Moscow's public argument against proliferation, namely, the notion that nuclear spread would be a contagious, virulent phenomenon, and the thesis that a world of nuclear powers would be precariously unstable.

As a particular case in point, Soviet allusions to the indivisibility of the proliferation threat would have us believe that Moscow regards all nuclear spread as equally dangerous, destabilizing, and contagious regardless of who acquires nuclear weapons or how large the resultant capability may be. Pushed to its logical extreme, this line of argument suggests that Soviet planners would view nuclear accession by "revanchist" West Germany and by a neutral and relatively benign state such as Sweden—both clearly nuclear threshold powers—with equal alarm. It also implies that should a state such as Sweden for any reason decide to go nuclear, that decision would immediately trigger pressures for proliferation to West Germany, Israel, and any other aspirant atomic power. Yet, if the French development of an operational nuclear force has failed to heighten Bonn's incentive for a similar capability, then it is certainly hard to imagine how Sweden's accession to nuclear status would even remotely threaten to do so. And it clearly taxes credulity to consider that the Soviets would regard a Swedish and a West German nuclear capability with similar apprehension when everybody fully recognizes that Moscow has long viewed West Germany as an overwhelmingly greater source of concern.

Why, then, have the Soviets advanced a declaratory "line" on the proliferation issue which so plainly glosses over these important distinctions? One seems compelled either to conclude that the Soviets have radically misperceived the objective realities of the proliferation problem, or to suspect that their public policy line has not altogether reflected their true assessment of the problem. In view of the growing sophistication which Moscow has displayed both in its intellectual approach to defense policy problems and in its general perspectives on the international system, it would seem highly unlikely that the Soviets have completely misperceived the problem.[20] In order to come to some understanding of how the Soviets in fact appraise the proliferation threat and accommodate it in their policy outlook, we must examine their public statements on the subject within the larger context of Soviet strategic perceptions, interests, and priorities.

## Moscow's Pragmatic Threat Appraisal

It is a common fact of international political discourse that states neither consistently say what they mean, mean what they say, nor reveal the entirety of their policy calculations to their intended public audiences. The various forms of public statements issued by a state are all geared to the practical considerations of enhancing the public image of the state, providing the most effective rationale for that state's external policies, and maximizing the prospect that those policies will achieve their intended objectives. This applies to Soviet propaganda no less than to that of any other country. In the case of the proliferation problem, much of Moscow's commentary has been focused on the im-

[20] A discussion of this growing "maturity" which has become evident in Moscow's foreign policy style may be found in William Zimmerman, *Soviet Perspectives on International Relations: 1956–1967* (Princeton, N.J.: Princeton University Press, 1969).

mediate matter of getting the NPT negotiated, concluded, and implemented. It has told us that the Soviets
are interested in nonproliferation and that they regard international acceptance of the NPT as a matter
of some importance to them. What it has not given us,
however, is any great insight into the various factors
which have motivated that interest, nor about the way
in which Soviet planners have privately assessed the
proliferation threat as a likely determinant of Soviet
foreign and strategic policy.

One reason for this is that the broad thrust of Moscow's public commentary has been closely harnessed
to its diplomatic pursuit of the Nonproliferation Treaty
and, as such, has primarily served political rather
than analytical purposes. Any elaborate public Soviet
discussion of hierarchical distinctions among various
possible forms of nuclear spread would merely weaken
the force of Moscow's arguments regarding the need
for universal acceptance of the NPT and, at the same
time, tarnish the image of Soviet disarmament "sin-
cerity" by implying a discriminatory double standard
in Moscow's nonproliferation policy. Not only would
such a public stance tend to condone implicitly the
spread of nuclear weapons to areas where it might be
deemed relatively "tolerable," it would also be anything but conducive to the willing acceptance of the
NPT by those countries singled out as being the most
"threatening." Nonetheless, the fact that the Soviet
Union's disarmament oratory has largely failed to advance any discrete typology of relative proliferation
threats—a typology whose existence in the minds of
Soviet strategic planners would seem virtually self-
evident—underscores the limited usefulness of Mos-

cow's propaganda rhetoric as a source of insight into the more important and relevant aspects of the proliferation problem.

This is not to imply that everything the Soviets have said in the disarmament forum has been merely diplomatic window dressing. However, when we examine Moscow's treatment of the problem within the larger context of Soviet strategic policy, some interesting divergencies appear.

In contrast to Moscow's rather alarmist and unvaried public stance, we can perhaps describe the real Soviet perception of the proliferation problem as pragmatic and hierarchical. This perception, while indeed no less concerned with the problem, reflects a measured rationality. It recognizes that nuclear dispersion is not, as publicly advertised, imminently threatening; that proliferation would be dangerous for the Soviet Union and for international security only to the degree that it posed a credible capability and propensity for significant troublemaking; and, therefore, that there do in fact exist distinguishable levels of proliferation tolerability and likelihood, each of which must be assessed and accommodated in terms of its own particular circumstances.

To be sure, this extraction of Moscow's presumed "realistic" assessment of the proliferation problem is largely speculative. Given the secrecy of Soviet political processes and the often limited reliability of Soviet source materials, any attempt to glean the private attitudes of the Kremlin's decision-makers must necessarily recognize a considerable margin of uncertainty. In the absence of reliable data, we often must resort to deductive modes of analysis and presumptive judgments using such ordering concepts as "stability," "equilibrium," "mutual deterrence," and the like—concepts which have become standard fare in western strategic thinking, yet which the Soviets themselves rarely use and which, in fact, may not even reflect how the Soviets intellectually approach their own strategic problems. Consequently, there is the ever-present danger of constructing speculative and detached models which may well be entirely logical and internally consistent in themselves, yet which may or may not really tell us what we need to know about how the problem actually bears on Soviet policy-making.

On the other hand, it seems an accepted assumption that the Soviet Union formulates its policies predominantly in terms of what it considers to be its broader "enlightened self-interest." And to the extent that we do know something about the character of this Soviet self-interest—for example, Moscow's desire to preserve the existing international status quo between the superpowers and its interest in keeping the danger of nuclear war within manageable proportions—we at least have a reasonable point of departure for making inferences about how the Soviets view the proliferation threat. Within limits, we can then test these inferences against various examples from past Soviet statements and behavior.

## SOVIET INCENTIVES FOR NONPROLIFERATION

Apart from its natural disinclination to share the prerogatives of nuclear power status with other states, the Soviet Union's opposition to nuclear dispersion has been motivated by a number of pragmatic considerations involving its most basic policy and security interests. The Soviet leaders have been obliged to recognize that "the secret of manufacturing nuclear weapons has virtually ceased to be a secret,"[21] and that it is now within the capability of a number of lesser states to develop nuclear forces sufficient to threaten the security of even the most powerful nations. In 1958, when Soviet-American nuclear dominance in the international arena was at its zenith, Khrushchev could easily scoff at the notion that a minor country might challenge that superpower ascendancy. "Aggression by a small country against a larger power," he asserted then, "is, in general, impossible."[22] With the increased availability of nuclear weapons technology and the possibility, however remote, that this technology could be wielded irresponsibly, the Soviets more recently have been forced to admit that even states "with limited nuclear stocks could inflict substantial damage on a stronger neighbor," and that "while this would be suicidal, such acts are not unknown."[23]

Moscow's concern that a multinuclear world might easily slip out of control and raise the explosive potential of the international system stems directly from a basic precept of Soviet strategic policy, namely, that a relatively stable, bipolar, mutual deterrence arrange-

[21] V. Shestov, "Major Success for the Cause of Peace," *International Affairs* (Moscow), no. 8 (August 1968).

[22] N. S. Khrushchev, letter to President Eisenhower, TASS International Service, August 5, 1958.

[23] Major General N. Talenskii, "The 'Absolute Weapon' and the Problem of Security," *International Affairs* (Moscow), no. 4 (April 1962), p. 36.

ment between the superpowers provides the most reliable framework for maintaining international security and keeping down the risks of nuclear war. During the 1960s, and particularly since the Cuban missile crisis of 1962, the Soviet Union has come to accept and find a measure of security in certain mutually recognized strategic nuclear "rules of the game" between the two superpowers. These rules derive from the capability of each to inflict unacceptable damage on the other even after having sustained a surprise first strike, from the general inability of either power to alter this standoff significantly by additional weapons deployments, and from the relative insensitivity of this balance to external "system shocks" which might be induced by the familiar array of present international forces. In other words, the Soviet Union has increasingly found the contemporary strategic milieu both manageable and generally satisfactory, and it consequently places a high premium on preserving the nuclear status quo. To the Soviets any further proliferation would alter that status quo by introducing new imponderables and "unknowns."

A brief survey of Soviet diplomacy during the Taiwan Strait crisis of 1958, when the outlines of the proliferation problem were still only barely discernible, may help to illustrate the nature of these Soviet concerns. In 1957, apparently emboldened by Khrushchev's boasts of Soviet missile-nuclear superiority over the West, Mao Tse-tung embarked on a policy of increasingly intractable militancy toward the United States. This militancy was marked initially by mounting verbal pyrotechnics from Peking deprecating the dangers of nuclear war and culminated in Communist

China's attempt to wrest the offshore island of Quemoy from Taiwan in the summer of 1958. For this endeavor, Mao sought the nuclear support that Khrushchev's advertised "superiority" seemed to offer.

Recognizing the enormous explosiveness of the situation and undoubtedly stirred by Mao's display of callous indifference to the prospect of nuclear escalation, the Soviets could not have responded with anything but alarm. They refused to grant Peking the public commitment of nuclear support until it was already clear to everyone that the crisis would abate. In the broader perspective, the Soviets were rudely awakened to the ominous possibility that in some future crisis, in which China possessed its own atomic bombs, the way out might not be so easy, and Moscow might then be dragged into a catalytic nuclear confrontation with the United States because of some irresponsibility on the part of its allies in Peking. The result is a matter of historical record. In the light of its already strained relations with Peking, the Soviet Union reassessed its commitments to the Sino-Soviet alliance and in 1959 terminated its nuclear aid program to Peking.[24] All of Moscow's disarmament policies subsequent to the Taiwan Strait imbroglio—including its proposals for nuclear free zones in Asia, its endorsement of the Test Ban Treaty in 1963, and its pursuit of NPT—have reflected a clear-cut Soviet decision both to

[24] For a detailed discussion of Moscow's role in this confrontation, see John R. Thomas, "Soviet Behavior in the Quemoy Crisis of 1958," *Orbis*, vol. VI, no. 1 (Spring 1962), pp. 38–64. See also Harold C. Hinton, *Soviet Response to Sino-American Crises: Chinese Expectations* (Research Paper P-298; Arlington, Va.: Institute for Defense Analyses, January 1967).

contain and isolate China's nuclear weapons program and to sacrifice the imperatives of Sino-Soviet "fraternal comradeship" in the larger interests of international stability and security.[25]

This reference to the Taiwan Strait crisis does not mean that Moscow's proliferation concerns were inspired exclusively, or even initially, by the "China factor," nor should it be taken to suggest that the current Sino-Soviet estrangement is wholly a product of Soviet unease over Peking's alleged "nuclear irresponsibility." Its purpose has simply been to illuminate Moscow's underlying attitude toward the dangers which might pervade a world laden with nuclear weapons. The Kremlin found the dangers controllable during the Taiwan episode because the *agent provocateur* then lacked the means to touch off a nuclear spark. It is the specter of some similar crisis in the future—in the Middle East, perhaps, or on the Asian subcontinent —in which the local protagonist *would* have nuclear arms that currently inspires Moscow's desire to put the brakes on further proliferation.

Finally, there is the possibility that the introduction of nuclear weaponry into conflict-prone regions might provoke a situation in which one possessor state would wield atomic weapons against its neighboring adversary. Indeed, a significant source of Moscow's proliferation concern centers on the various middle-level nuclear threshold nations—countries which have attained some measure of regional stature, which either

[25] In an NBC-sponsored interview almost three years after his ouster, Khrushchev gave himself credit for having "maintained world peace" because of his refusal to supply nuclear weapons to Communist China. *New York Times,* June 27, 1967.

possess or are within reach of the economic and technical preconditions for mounting a nuclear force, and which may be encouraged to exercise this nuclear option by local events impinging on their own strategic interests. Unlike such present nuclear states as France and China, whose nuclear capabilities have stemmed mainly from pretensions to great-power status, these nations derive their nuclear incentives predominantly from regional insecurities and disagreements not directly related to any broader interests in competing with the superpowers. Their pressures to consider developing nuclear weapons largely emanate either from beliefs that a nuclear capacity might reduce their need to rely on the support of their respective superpower benefactors, from expectations that a nuclear posture might offer them a decisive military edge over their local adversaries, or from reciprocal fears that their enemies might preempt them in developing atomic arms.

All of these incentives imply manifold challenges to the prospects for international stability. One can easily visualize, for example, how nuclear proliferation to such an unstable region as the Middle East might well create inducements to local troublemaking which do not now exist in the absence of indigenous nuclear arsenals. As one Soviet article put it, "the emergence of new nuclear powers would increase regional tensions and aggravate the danger of nuclear war."[26] A situation could conceivably develop in which a newly arrived nuclear power (say, Israel), perceiving its most vital security interests to be in imminent danger, would

[26] Nikolayev and Shestov, "Decisive Round at Geneva," p. 7.

find much to be gained and virtually nothing to be lost by unleashing nuclear blows against its adversary. In such an event, the "nuclear taboo" which the two superpowers have so carefully cultivated during the 1960s would instantly be abrogated, and the floodgates would then be opened to all sorts of escalatory pressures which could threaten to draw Washington and Moscow into a head-on collision.

Despite all of the apparent soul-searching in recent years over whether or not local wars involving nuclear weapons would "inevitably" escalate to a global thermonuclear war, it remains a vital preconception both of Soviet strategic doctrine and of Soviet foreign policy that, in such an event, the pressures for escalation would be indeed compelling. A rare comment in the Soviet professional military literature on the proliferation issue reflects this preconception: "Suppose nuclear weapons came into the hands of two countries hostile to one another? What guarantee is there that one of them would not use them against the other? As is well known, the heat of passion is great even in local conflicts, and in such a conflict where nuclear weapons are used other nuclear powers could well become involved."[27]

Yet even though the Soviets would undoubtedly prefer no additional nuclear dispersion of any sort, they still have to face the twin realities that numerous countries are capable of developing independent nuclear arsenals and that the various internal political, economic, and strategic considerations which could motivate those countries to go nuclear imply varying con-

[27] L. Zavialov, "In the Interests of All People," *Krasnaia zvezda,* June 25, 1968.

sequences for Soviet national interests. In practical terms, therefore, the Soviet Union would seem obliged to consider each category of potential nuclear diffusion on its individual merits and assign that category a relative level of priority in the over-all Soviet proliferation-threat spectrum. That Moscow in fact does hold such a hierarchical view of the proliferation problem has been suggested in a number of Soviet press statements. Departing from the general Soviet public tendency to describe all forms of proliferation as equally undesirable, *Izvestiia*'s Vikenty Matveyev suggested that while it is indeed desirable for the NPT to be accepted by all countries, "a simple arithmetical approach to this question is insufficient. *The most important thing is to exclude the possibility of the acquisition of nuclear weapons by those circles that have expansionist and revanchist aims of recarving existing state borders. . . .*"[28] While Matveyev chose not to specify the "expansionist" and "revanchist" states he had in mind, a *Pravda* commentary shortly after the NPT signing observed that the ratification of the treaty by West Germany, South Africa, and Israel—all full-fledged "revanchist" powers in the Soviet lexicon—was being awaited in Moscow with "special" anticipation.[29]

Such assertions, coupled with the "common-sense"

[28] "Let Us Advance Further," *Izvestiia*, July 3, 1968 (emphasis added).

[29] G. Ratiani, "The Half-Year Mark," *Pravda*, July 7, 1968. Similarly, V. Popov spoke of a "nuclear itch" in Bonn, Tel Aviv, and Pretoria and observed: "Thus in the center of Europe, in the Near East, and in South Africa, seeds are being plowed into the soil, seeds which may produce dangerous crops." "Nuclear Weapons and Security," *Krasnaia zvezda*, May 31, 1968.

probability that some nuclear-armed states would simply be more prone to troublemaking than others, provide a strong basis for assuming that the Soviet Union in fact accepts a much more discriminating view of alternative forms of nuclear diffusion than much of its propaganda rhetoric would indicate. Without attempting any detailed inquiry into the likely breakdown of such a Soviet proliferation threat hierarchy, we can briefly suggest that Moscow's private assessment of the over-all problem includes at least three general categories. Starting with the least significant level of threat, the first category would include forms of proliferation whose consequences for international stability would, at worst, be only marginally significant. This category would include nuclear access by such stable and politically quiescent countries as Canada, Sweden, and Switzerland, none of which would be likely to use nuclear weapons for acquisitive or provocative purposes. The general Soviet response to nuclear weapons access by any country in this category would, aside from propaganda outbursts criticizing the "bad example" set for other states, most probably be one of quiet toleration and general unconcern.

The second, and less tolerable, category would include the acquisition of atomic weapons by those volatile and conflict-prone threshold countries located in such troubled areas of the world as the Middle East and Asia. This would clearly be contrary to the Soviet Union's foreign policy interests because of the heightened regional instabilities it would undoubtedly produce. The Soviet reaction would most likely be one not merely of verbal disapprobation but of concerted economic and diplomatic sanctions against the offending power as well. Yet even in the event of this sort of nuclear diffusion, the more vital security interests of the Soviet Union would be unlikely to be compromised, and Moscow, however grudgingly, could probably learn to live with the situation. International relations would undoubtedly assume new levels of tension, but they would not, in all likelihood, become totally unmanageable by the superpowers.

The third and final category of proliferation would be limited to those economically developed and strategically significant threshold countries whose acquisition of a nuclear delivery capability would be clearly and categorically unacceptable to Moscow. Such countries are those whose possession of nuclear weapons would immediately endanger the physical security of the Soviet Union or would directly threaten Moscow's most jealously guarded external policy interests. The obvious—and most likely exclusive—case in point here is West Germany. The Soviet Union has long been acutely sensitive to the prospect of an atomic arsenal within the reach of its former wartime enemy and has left no room for ambiguity about it. An official Soviet government note issued in 1963 in protest against the proposed NATO multilateral nuclear force, for example, emphatically stated that "no matter how nuclear weapons fall into the hands of the Bundeswehr, directly or indirectly, the Soviet Union would regard this as an immediate threat to its vital national interests and would be obliged to take the necessary measures dictated by the circumstances."[30] Soviet Foreign Minister

[30] Soviet government note of February 5, 1963, *Pravda*, February 8, 1963.

Gromyko displayed a similar conviction in his address to the Twenty-third CPSU Congress when he observed that "the Soviet Union and its friends will never re-sign themselves to plans to give the Federal Republic of Germany access to nuclear weapons."[31] And Pre-mier Kosygin could not have been more categorical in his steadfast opposition to West German nuclear acquisition than in his statement that "as for the FRG, I must say that it will have to join the agreement on nonproliferation whether it wants to or not. We will not allow the FRG to have nuclear weapons and will take all measures to prevent it from obtaining the pos-sibility of possessing these weapons. *We say this with full determination.*"[32]

How the Soviets would respond to a West German nuclear capability is now a moot point, however, because of Bonn's recent acceptance of the Nonpro-liferation Treaty. Similarly, the problems raised by nuclear proliferation to the "nonprovocative" states have also, at least for the moment, become academic since the important nuclear threshold countries in that category have likewise acceded to the treaty.

It is the possibility of nuclear spread occurring in the second category which currently keeps the pro-liferation issue a lively topic of concern for the Soviets, since three of the major threshold powers in that class —India, Pakistan, and Israel—have remained decidedly adamant in their reluctance to sign the NPT, and their

[31] A. A. Gromyko, speech to the Twenty-third Congress of the CPSU, TASS International Service, April 2, 1966.

[32] Remarks by Premier Kosygin at a London news conference, February 9, 1967, cited in *Pravda*, February 11, 1967 (emphasis added).

cooperation is very important if the treaty is to have any practical meaning.

Until those states indicate an explicit willingness to renounce their nuclear options, the threat of nuclear spread will continue to pose tangible problems for the Soviet Union. Premier Kosygin may have been correct when he observed that general acceptance of the NPT would be "convincing proof that states are capable of finding mutually acceptable solutions to complicated international problems."[33] Still, it remains clear that the reluctant threshold countries will somehow have to be persuaded to accept the treaty before that proof can be significantly realized. Until then, as one American analyst candidly reflected, the NPT will have done little more than expose "the fact that the United States and the Soviet Union can be equally pious when obliging themselves to refrain from doing something they would not have done in any event."[34] Two questions therefore arise: First, why have these important threshold countries so far balked at signing the Nonproliferation Treaty? And second, how does their recalcitrance bear on the Soviet Union's broader arms control policies and imperatives?

## THE PROLIFERATION FACTOR IN SOVIET ARMS CONTROL POLICY-MAKING

In the simplest terms, the threshold countries that have declined to sign the NPT have taken that stance

[33] Speech by A. N. Kosygin at ceremony for signing the Nuclear Nonproliferation Treaty, TASS International Service, July 1, 1968.

[34] Bader, *The United States and the Spread of Nuclear Weapons,* p. 102.

because (1) they are unwilling to renounce their nuclear options in the absence of credible substitute guarantees of their security by the superpowers; (2) they believe their regional security problems demand a measure of military self-sufficiency; and (3) they suspect that the superpowers have been trying to have the best of two worlds by denying others access to atomic weapons while at the same time even more firmly establishing their own nuclear ascendancy.[35] Because of their understandable insistence on equity and reciprocity, these countries are disinclined to submit to measures of self-denial without some sort of simultaneous *quid pro quo* from the superpowers in curbing their own nuclear arms race. After all, if the United States and the Soviet Union, in the interests of "international stability," are truly opposed to nuclear spread, then it should certainly be incumbent upon them to make good that commitment by observing a measure of self-restraint themselves.

For these reasons, it is of particular interest that Moscow chose to voice its appeal for bilateral Soviet-American strategic arms limitation talks on the very eve of the signing of the Nonproliferation Treaty.[36]

[35] Many of these threshold countries who have *signed* the NPT, moreover, have done so on the specific condition that the superpowers attend to the matter of restraining their own arms race as well. The Japanese government, for example, has made it quite clear that before formally ratifying its acceptance of the treaty, it "will pay particular attention to developments in the disarmament negotiations." Philip Shabecoff, "Nonnuclear Pact Signed by Japan," *New York Times*, February 4, 1970.

[36] There had been earlier rumors that Moscow was preparing to accept the U.S. offer to discuss a strategic weapons limitation agreement held out by President Johnson in his January 1967 State

No doubt Moscow's recognition of the emergent East-West nuclear parity relationship as a promising basis for such talks, and its concern over the insecurities and economic burdens which a new round in the arms race would impose on the Soviet Union, played a dominant role in influencing the decision. However, the timing of the announcement suggests that Moscow's concern over the proliferation threat may have been a significant factor as well. The Soviets knew that several nuclear threshold states would insist on a demonstration of superpower good faith toward the cause of disarmament as a precondition to their own acceptance of the treaty. Moscow may well have calculated that, by capitalizing on the momentum and the spirit of international optimism established by the NPT's conclusion, a declaration of Soviet willingness to entertain strategic arms control talks would be cast in the best possible light, and, at the same time, provide the reluctant threshold countries with every possible incentive to accept the treaty.

To dispel any residual fears that the treaty was merely a reflection of Soviet-American superpower collusion to bolster their common interests at the expense of other countries, Soviet propaganda took great pains to point out the continued intractability of the American "imperialists" and defended the Nonproliferation Treaty singularly as an expression of Soviet interest in its own security and in the cause of peace. One commentator put it quite bluntly:

---

of the Union address. The official announcement of this Soviet acceptance, however, did not come until just prior to the NPT signing, in a speech by Foreign Minister Gromyko to the Supreme Soviet. TASS International Service, June 27, 1968.

You can see how stupid it is to talk about any collusion between the Soviet Union and the United States. We cannot expand our cooperation until Washington stops its aggression. There are no signs of rapprochement between us. . . . The Soviet Union regards the treaty as a major success of its foreign policy, for all the socialist countries, and for all other forces of peace. It is advantageous to the socialist cause, so when we agreed to sign the nuclear nonproliferation treaty we did not have any conciliation with the United States in mind. We were seeing to the interests of the socialist countries and wanted to block the nuclear arms drive.[37]

Soviet pronouncements also frequently voiced the general theme that the Soviet Union "takes very seriously the treaty on the nonproliferation of nuclear weapons when it says that with good will, talks will take place concerning effective measures for stopping the nuclear arms race."[38] To the extent that the Soviets generally have attached high priority to the proliferation question in their disarmament agenda, there is

[37] G. Shakhov, Radio Moscow, International Service, June 18, 1968. That this "indictment" of the United States was largely linked to Soviet efforts to gain support for the NPT by the nonnuclear states is further suggested by the fact that the Soviets were showing conciliatory signs elsewhere. Vikenty Matveyev, for example, observed that "there is a growing and quite influential and serious movement in the United States, even among authoritative political leaders, in favor of a restraint on the arms race," and that "the situation, though a complex one, is nevertheless one in which one can seek realistic, practical steps in the field of disarmament from the ruling circles of the United States." Radio Moscow, Domestic Service, June 30, 1968.

[38] Viktor Glazunov, Radio Moscow, International Service, July 1, 1968. Similarly, party leader Brezhnev described the Soviet strategic arms control gesture as a demonstration of "good faith"

little doubt that they have considered this "good will" to mean evidence of satisfactory progress in the direction of curbing nuclear spread.

Yet while Moscow has insisted on such progress toward nonproliferation, it has also been obliged to recognize that the problem of halting nuclear dispersion is not altogether a one-way affair. The Soviet Union and the United States have together borne a considerable burden of the efforts to make nonproliferation a realistic possibility, both through having come to terms on the NPT and by having agreed to seek ways of restraining their own nuclear-missile arms competition. The very conclusion of the Nonproliferation Treaty itself must be considered as a significant first step in the right direction, and the superpowers' recognition of the need to get on with the more serious matter of heading off a dangerous new spiral in their own arms race quite likely had a good deal of influence in persuading many of those countries who had initially voiced their concerns over this arms race ultimately to sign the NPT. Nevertheless, the Soviet Union must somehow reconcile its asserted desire for universal acceptance of the NPT with the demands of various threshold states for additional superpower concessions as a precondition to their own nuclear abstinence. In addition, the Soviet Union must recognize both the possibility that some of these countries may continue to see certain incentives for going nuclear despite any concessions the superpowers may make, and the hard reality that even universal NPT ratification provides,

toward "strengthening universal peace." Speech at a Soviet-Hungarian friendship meeting in the Kremlin, Radio Moscow, Domestic Service, July 3, 1968.

in the end, no real guarantee against eventual proliferation.

To note this problem, of course, is hardly to suggest either that the Soviets are singularly obsessed by the threat of nuclear dispersion or that the proliferation factor in any way commits Moscow to a strategic arms control policy toward the United States which it would otherwise refrain from pursuing. In fact, the whole question of nuclear proliferation has increasingly become a matter of second-order importance to the Soviets in light of West Germany's acceptance of the NPT. Bonn's formal rejection of the nuclear option has eroded substantially the leading proliferation challenge to Soviet security interests and has removed the main proliferation-related impediment against serious Soviet-American nuclear arms limitation negotiations.

At the same time, however, the Soviet Union cannot wholly dismiss the residual prospects of nuclear acquisition by other, less cooperative, threshold countries. Israel, for example, promises to remain firmly against signing the NPT so long as it perceives its security to be endangered by the intransigence of its volatile Arab adversaries and so long as the Soviet Union continues to fuel that Arab intransigence through policies of military aid and moral encouragement. India, for its part, has made it clear that further security guarantees from the superpowers will have to be forthcoming before it will consider acceding to the NPT. And it seems highly unlikely that Pakistan will accede to the treaty so long as its Indian adversary refuses to do so. Each of these three countries, in other words, will probably withhold endorsement of the NPT until some sort of reciprocal concessions are forthcoming from the superpowers. Consequently, insofar as the Soviet Union seriously hopes to further circumscribe the proliferation problem, it will have to show a greater willingness to accommodate the interests of the threshold states than it has thus far evinced. And on this score, Moscow appears decidedly reluctant.

In particular, if those states presently holding out on signing the treaty should continue to insist on visible, explicit, and credible defense commitments from the superpowers, then the prospects for keeping the nuclear club restricted to its present membership will be slim indeed.[39] The Soviet Union has been willing to "solemnly confirm" its promise to aid "any nonnuclear signatory of the treaty who becomes the victim of aggression or threatened aggression with the use of nuclear weapons."[40] At the same time, it has been distinctly unwilling to commit itself to anything beyond this rather vague formulation. Those countries on the receiving end of this guarantee may understandably be less than impressed with the "solemnity" of Moscow's pledge, and may insist—as an Indian delegate to the U.N. Disarmament Commission did in 1965—that "nations are not interested in having another Hiroshima on their soil before an assurance of this nature could come into effect."[41] Yet the Soviet leaders have

[39] For a general discussion of the extreme difficulties and complexities posed by the problem of security guarantees, see Mason Willrich, "Guarantees to Non-Nuclear Nations," *Foreign Affairs*, vol. 44, no. 4 (July 1966), pp. 683–92.

[40] *Izvestiia*, June 19, 1968.

[41] Statement by the Indian representative (Chakravarty) to the U.N. Disarmament Commission, May 4, 1965, *Documents on Disarmament, 1965* (Washington, D.C.: U.S. Arms Control and Disarmament Agency, 1966), p. 148.

given every indication that they have no intention of becoming entangled in any regional defense commitments which, in a crisis, might limit their flexibility, foreclose their options, or otherwise compromise their own interests. Moscow's sobering experience during the Taiwan Strait affair in 1958 and its seemingly inexorable embroilment in the current Arab-Israeli morass have undoubtedly underscored the desirability of keeping a healthy distance from the narrow interests of its more mercurial clients.

Beyond this understandable calculus of realpolitik, Soviet statements have also argued that explicit superpower security guarantees to the nonnuclear states would, in practice, be virtually the same thing as expanding the existing military alliance system of the two opposing camps and would, therefore, only heighten the intractability of East-West relations. *Pravda*, for example, reported that "some have proposed that the nuclear powers, at their choosing and using their judgment, give a direct guarantee to any country they wished. Such an act, however, would impose a deeper split in the world and would turn the globe into a system of antagonistic nuclear groupings."[42]

The general Soviet approach on this point has been to rationalize its negative attitude toward guarantees

[42] M. Maratov, *Pravda*, June 16, 1968. See also the similar comment by S. Beglov: "If someone wishes to whisper to the non-nuclear countries the idea of some kind of 'automatic' mechanism for guaranteeing the interests of their security, or in the utilization of the atom for peace, and of some kind of method of meeting these interests outside the framework of collaboration between the nuclear and non-nuclear countries stipulated by the treaty, then he is doing a disservice both to the non-nuclear countries and to the cause of peace throughout the world." "The Treaty Is on Its Way," *Izvestiia*, September 28, 1968.

by pointing out an even less desirable alternative: "It is patently obvious that any guarantee is better than general nuclear rearmament."[43] In fact, in their more vocal pronouncements on the matter of security guarantees, the Soviets have even gone so far as to assert the paternalistic argument that the nonnuclear powers really have little reason to complain. Yuri Zhukov clearly implied as much in a 1968 *Pravda* commentary:

> It is said that if an agreement on the nonproliferation of nuclear weapons is not accompanied by precise security pledges by those countries already possessing them . . . then this would only legalize the division of the world into nuclear and nonnuclear states and would allow the nuclear powers to increase supplies of their weapons and to improve them. But now, when there is no agreement, do not nuclear powers still have the capability of continuing to produce their armaments? And is anybody unaware of the actual situation, which is that five powers are already producing nuclear bombs? So then—will it be better if another dozen countries engage in their production.[44]

Thus, it seems that the Soviet Union will not go beyond certain limits in accommodating the more strident objections to the NPT held by such threshold states as India. For example, Moscow will hardly rush into a program of sizable strategic force reductions solely because some lesser proliferation-prone countries demand "not only the prevention of further proliferation but also the reversal of present proliferation."[45] Similarly, the Soviets will probably continue to view explicit

[43] Maratov, *Pravda*, June 16, 1968.
[44] "Traps," *Pravda*, December 8, 1968.
[45] Statement by the Indian representative, *Documents on Disarmament, 1965*, p. 147.

security guarantees to these states as an unacceptable price to pay for nonproliferation. And finally, if past experience in assessing Soviet behavior is any guide, Moscow will almost certainly not elect to submit Soviet nuclear facilities to any close on-site inspection as a necessary *quid pro quo* for some state's nuclear self-abnegation, no matter how "international" the inspection team might be. Khrushchev once described such Soviet facilities as "sacred places where not even all friends are admitted,"[46] and, given the Soviet Union's traditional obsession with secrecy and societal closure, there is little chance that Moscow will change its attitude on this matter in the foreseeable future.

## Problems and Prospects

What, then, if the Soviet Union's efforts for universal acceptance of the Nonproliferation Treaty fail? How will Moscow then view the resultant implications both for its own policies and for the international system as a whole? It is important to recognize, as the Soviets themselves no doubt do, that a state's reluctance or refusal to sign the NPT does not, in itself, mean that that state's eventual nuclear acquisition is a foregone conclusion. Just as the Soviet Union is politically indisposed to grant specific military security guarantees to the various nuclear threshold countries, so might those latter countries also be constrained by certain internal political injunctions against accepting the Nonproliferation Treaty. One can easily imagine, for example, how various powerful factions within the Israeli government

[46] Speech at a Soviet-Czechoslovak friendship meeting, Radio Moscow, July 12, 1958.

might persuasively argue that Tel Aviv's acceptance of the NPT prior to a stable settlement in the Middle East situation would risk giving up a vital psycho-political ace in the hole.

We can speculate, in fact, that the Soviet Union may be placing its hopes for nonproliferation to a considerable degree precisely on the restraints imposed by *internal* disincentives within the various threshold states against exercising their nuclear options. For one thing, it is not at all inconceivable that in the course of their budget deliberations, the various threshold countries might well find the prestige value of nuclear weapons offset by the massive economic costs which would be involved in developing a militarily significant nuclear capability. There are other injunctions which might similarly militate against what would otherwise seem eminently reasonable arguments for various states to go nuclear. These injunctions vary widely according to the particular political, military, and psychological pressures bearing on the different threshold countries and need not be examined in detail here. Suffice it to say that on close examination, the superficial persuasiveness of the French proposition that "one is nuclear or one is negligible"[47] must indeed have a hollow appeal to many of the presently nuclear-capable nations. The leaders of threshold states are certainly aware of the possible costs of membership in the nuclear community: the increased vulnerability to retaliation; the vast drain on scarce national resources; and

[47] French Defense Minister Pierre Messmer, *Journal officiel* (Paris), January 24, 1963, cited in B. W. Augenstein, "The Chinese and French Programs for the Development of National Nuclear Forces," *Orbis*, vol. XI, no. 3 (Fall 1967), p. 854.

the potential erosion of any relationship their state might enjoy with its superpower benefactor.

As one American scholar has suggested, "it is possible that 'independent' nuclear capabilities will lose attraction for those states which are willing to calculate costs and benefits."[48]

Even if all the Soviet Union's policy accommodations and powers of diplomatic persuasion, U.S. efforts, and compelling internal disincentives within the various threshold states should fail to prevent further nuclear spread, it is still not at all certain that the prospects for East-West agreement and international stability would perforce become consigned to the stable of lost causes. With the exception of West Germany, it is highly unlikely that any newly emergent nuclear power could—at least in the 1970s—seriously complicate Soviet strategic planning or significantly undermine Soviet security. Even the relatively sophisticated French nuclear *force de frappe*, with its attendant array of supersonic bombers and medium-range missiles, has been described by Soviet spokesmen as far too modest ever to be "in a position to change the balance of power in the world."[49] Not only have the Soviets seemed wholly satisfied with their ability to deter this force, they have spoken confidently about the impossibility of its even getting through Soviet defenses, much less causing any damage: "We can easily

[48] Richard N. Rosecrance, "International Stability and Nuclear Diffusion," *The Dispersion of Nuclear Weapons*, ed. Richard N. Rosecrance (New York: Columbia University Press, 1964), p. 312.

[49] Nekrasov, "Contrary to the Times and to Good Sense," *Pravda*, January 19, 1963.

imagine how vulnerable these means of attack are, and there is no doubt that the destruction of these planes would be followed by reprisals from tremendously superior forces."[50]

Similarly, for all their scathing criticism of Peking's nuclear ambitions, the Soviets have displayed remarkably little concern over the immediate threat potential of Communist China's atomic capability. "Just because they have a few bombs or have conducted a few tests does not mean that they are strong in modern rocketry. In order to have such strength it is necessary to have many types of missile delivery systems, electronic equipment, and so forth. It is very difficult for China's weak economy to bring all these about solely by relying on its own efforts."[51] Even though the Chinese have displayed an embryonic nuclear capability of some notable dimensions, the Soviets contend that the complexities of translating the mere capacity to detonate a nuclear "device" into a full-blown, strategically significant weapons-delivery capability are so enormous that it most likely will be a number of years in the future before Peking's nuclear posture will warrant serious Soviet concern for the country's security.[52]

[50] Radio Moscow, International Service, December 11, 1963. For additional discussion of Moscow's attitudes regarding the French nuclear force, see Thomas W. Wolfe, *Soviet Commentary on the French "Force de Frappe"* (RM-4359-ISA; Santa Monica, Cal.: The RAND Corporation, January 1965).

[51] Talk by Colonel Miyev, "What Price Have the Chinese People Paid for Nuclear Testing?" Radio Moscow, to China, June 5, 1967.

[52] Shortly before the first Chinese nuclear test in late October 1964, Khrushchev hinted his anticipation that the test would be

On balance, the Soviets seem to recognize clearly that for nuclear proliferation—at least to the more underdeveloped and economically constrained threshold nations—to alter substantially the existing pattern of Soviet-American bipolar nuclear deterrence would require far greater capabilities than the mere ability to explode an atomic bomb, and that the likelihood of such capabilities being mounted by any of these nations in the near future is remote indeed.[53] Pending

---

soon forthcoming and added that he did not expect it would pose any immediate threat. This remark was made during an interview with Aichiro Fukiyama, a member of the Japanese Liberal-Democratic Party, and was reported by *Kyodo* (Tokyo), October 6, 1964. It should be strongly emphasized, however, that such Soviet professions of unconcern over the *immediate* dangers of China's nuclear capability do not in any way mean that the Soviet Union will be able to retain its composure once that capability reaches strategically significant proportions. Indeed, as chapter 4 will discuss in some detail, there are good reasons to believe that in the long run, China's nuclear posture will come to complicate Soviet defense planning a great deal. For the moment, Moscow's seemingly confident attitudes regarding the Chinese nuclear threat are probably not altogether unjustified, but in the larger perspective they must also be read as reflecting a detectable element of nervous whistling in the dark.

[53] Richard Rosecrance has advanced a rather useful theoretical "model" of the sort of proliferation threat calculus which we are attributing to the Soviets. For any new nuclear state to have a significant destabilizing effect on world politics, he has argued, it must display: (1) the economic and technical ability to build atomic bombs; (2) the capability to build or obtain supporting delivery systems and command-and-control facilities; (3) the willingness to acquire nuclear weapons; (4) the ability to avoid major power counteraction to nullify the advantages of its nuclear status; and (5) the actual exploitation of its nuclear capability to endanger local or international peace. "Failure to

the emergence of such capabilities, they seem quite willing to agree that "the destabilizing effects of nuclear diffusion at the strategic level will probably not outweigh the stabilizing effects" accruing from the deadlocked Soviet-American mutual deterrence relationship.[54]

The destabilizing potential of such diffusion at substrategic levels poses more immediate problems. As suggested before, however, the Soviet leaders probably temper their concerns over this threat with the recognition that internal disincentives may constrain the threshold countries from building the weapons in the first place. The Soviets also know that there are strong possibilities that the superpowers could cooperate tacitly in preventing local nuclear antagonists from getting out of line. And, finally, they are aware that if a threshold state goes nuclear and threatens to use atomic weapons in a regional crisis, the responsibility, restraint, and mutual deterrence of the two superpowers would perhaps help to decompress the situation and keep it from exploding into a dangerous Soviet-American strategic showdown.

Soviet arms control interests vis-à-vis the United States, it thus seems, will be influenced in more or less direct proportion to the degree that nuclear proliferation adversely affects the stability and manageability

pass through each of these five stages," he concludes, "means that nuclear diffusion does not attain to international significance; it does not pose an independent problem to world peace." Rosecrance, *The Dispersion of Nuclear Weapons*, p. 293.

[54] Robert W. Tucker, *Stability and the Nth Country Problem* (Special Studies Group Memorandum No. 5; Arlington, Va.: Institute for Defense Analyses, November 1961), p. 26.

of the international system. If, for any number of possible reasons, West Germany should ever abrogate the NPT and acquire an independent nuclear capability, the Soviet Union would no doubt perceive the event as a political-military challenge of such profound and immediate gravity that there would be no hopes for arms control and East-West détente. Barring that unlikely eventuality, however, there is little reason to believe that the prospects for arms control will be seriously threatened by the proliferation problem.[55] It is significant that the rather apocalyptic pronouncements which so heavily dominated Moscow's commentary on the proliferation issue prior to the conclusion of the NPT have afterward appeared with progressive infrequency. Indeed, they have completely abated now that West Germany has formally renounced its nuclear option, which strongly suggests that Bonn's acceptance of the NPT (along with that of Japan and various other "critical" threshold countries)

[55] One tends to suspect, incidentally, that the more strident Soviet criticisms of Bonn's purported nuclear ambitions have been exaggerated out of all proportion to the realities of West German internal politics on the proliferation issue. A highly suggestive empirical study, based on extensive interview sampling of West German elite attitudes, has demonstrated that the desire for a nuclear capability has in fact been surprisingly low on the part of most political leaders in Bonn. See Karl W. Deutsch, *Arms Control and the Atlantic Alliance* (New York: John Wiley and Sons, 1967), pp. 50–57. As for the few remaining "pro-nuclear" German political figures, moreover, Soviet statements themselves have periodically expressed cautious expectations that the United States, as the responsible senior alliance partner in NATO, will "have enough firmness to give a definite 'no' to those Bonn politicians who still seek these weapons." Burlatskii, "Problems Affecting All Mankind."

has drastically diminished the immediate magnitude of the proliferation threat as perceived by the Soviets and has eliminated the major sources of Moscow's concern over the viability of the treaty itself. It also virtually confirms that the burden of Soviet declaratory statements on proliferation merely represented a propaganda adjunct of Moscow's pursuit of the NPT. Even though important threshold countries have still refrained from signing the treaty, Moscow's former preoccupation with the proliferation question appears today to have become all but forgotten as SALT moves increasingly to the forefront of Soviet arms control interest and activity.

It would be incorrect to conclude, of course, that the problem of nuclear dispersion has itself become a thing of the past. Those states which have thus far persisted in opposing the NPT will most likely continue to keep the proliferation issue alive for some time to come. Moreover, while Moscow would clearly be less than eager to see those countries in possession of nuclear arms, there are clear limits on its ability to have things its own way. Despite all the diplomatic exhortations which the Soviet Union may invoke against their nuclear ambitions, the simple fact remains that unless the recalcitrant threshold nations can be persuaded that it would be in their own best interests not to go nuclear, then the possibility of their nuclear accession will have to continue to be a variable in Soviet strategic planning. And in the event of such nuclear accession, there would probably be little the Soviets could do except learn to live with the situation. Yet the important point to be made is that none of these factors should be regarded as particularly threatening to the larger prospects for Soviet-American arms control accords. There is good reason to believe that while Soviet planners may ultimately find further nuclear diffusion inexorable, they will also come to find it tolerable—and even manageable—to a surprising degree. In what may have been one of the most revealing glimpses into the underlying "pragmatism" of Soviet thinking on this count, an *International Affairs* article asserted with almost sublime self-confidence: "[I]t is mainly the non-nuclear states that have an interest in the [nonproliferation] treaty being concluded, since in *the final account, the Soviet Union, being a mighty nuclear power, can itself guarantee its own security and that of its allies in the absence of such a treaty.*"[56]

The assumptions implicit in this statement are of central importance, it seems, in bringing Moscow's appraisal of the proliferation issue into its proper perspective vis-à-vis the larger issues currently facing Soviet strategy and arms control policy. Keeping the East-West nuclear balance free of precarious instabilities is a matter of enduring interest to both superpowers and remains far and away the most crucial imperative for continued international security. Consequently, despite the continued prospects for nuclear proliferation and the Soviet Union's manifest displeasure with those prospects, developments and interactions in the Soviet-American strategic relationship will most likely play the predominant role in determining Soviet arms control interests and priorities during the 1970s. In the short run, of course, while widespread nuclear dispersion remains a mere contingency rather than an

[56] Nikolayev and Shestov, "Decisive Round at Geneva," p. 5 (emphasis added).

114

accomplished fact, the "proliferation factor" will undoubtedly continue to motivate such Soviet disarmament proposals as a comprehensive test ban treaty, regional nuclear free zones, and the like. Yet in the longer run, in a world in which the nuclear club might well take in new members, the proliferation issue will probably become less a matter for disarmament debate than a tangible political-military problem to be recognized and accommodated. Moscow may well come to find itself resisting nuclear spread to some countries and tolerating it to others. In either case, the problem of strategic arms limitation will almost assuredly persist, and Soviet dispositions toward it will be determined less by the threat or the reality of nuclear dispersion than by perceptions of the U.S. adversary and by the more "traditional" factors examined in chapters 1 and 2, namely, economic incentives and constraints, "objective" strategic necessity, and internal political pressures and conflicts, all of which ultimately shape the contours of Soviet national security policy.

# 4

## The China Factor

NATURE OF THE CHINA FACTOR

CHINA HAS LONG BEEN the Soviet Union's most perplexing problem. The turmoil and erratic developments along the 4,000-mile Sino-Soviet frontier and throughout China during the past half-century have led the Soviet Union to adopt policies in regard to China that often were not consistent with one another or with its global policies and aims. Soviet policy toward China has reflected its traditional anxieties over border security as well as long-standing economic and strategic ambitions in China. For a time, Stalin seriously underestimated the speed and scope of the communist victory in China; the Soviets only belatedly became aware of the role a Communist China might play in world communism and of the potential significance of China in the post-World War II strategic balance.[1]

[1] According to Red Guard sources, Mao Tse-tung told the Chinese Communist Central Committee in 1962 that the Sino-Soviet conflict went back to 1945 "when Stalin tried to prevent the Chinese revolution by saying that there should not be any

After resolving their earlier doubts, the Soviets may since have seriously underestimated the divisive elements in the Sino-Soviet alliance.

Behind the Sino-Soviet split lie several decades of contradictory Soviet policies. The Soviets combined more or less conventional power politics with assistance and encouragement to such mutually hostile elements as various revolutionaries (e.g., Sun Yat-sen, Mao Tse-tung, assorted warlords, and dissident tribal regimes in border regions) and the established anti-revolutionary governments in Peking (until 1927), Nanking, and, during World War II, Chungking.[2] It

---

civil war and that we must collaborate with Chiang Kai-shek. . . . When did Stalin begin to have confidence in us? It began in the winter of 1950, during the Resist-America Aid-Korea campaign. . . ." See Mao Tse-tung, speech to the Tenth Plenary Session of the Eighth Central Committee, September 24, 1962, excerpted in *New York Times*, March 1, 1970. See also Donald S. Zagoria, *The Sino-Soviet Conflict, 1956–61* (Princeton, N.J.: Princeton University Press, 1962), Introduction, footnotes 9 and 11.

[2] Soviet broadcasts beamed at China have recently featured various commentaries on the history of Soviet assistance to China in which World War II military assistance to the Chungking government of Chiang Kai-shek is mentioned more prominently than the later assistance to Mao Tse-tung's regime. See, for example, the November 28, 1969, broadcast of Radio Peace and Progress (Moscow) which claimed that vast quantities of matériel, including nine hundred fighter aircraft were provided beginning in 1939 at a time when Britain and France allegedly created "barriers" to shipment of matériel through Burma and Indochina. Another such broadcast (the seventeenth in a series—see Radio Moscow, in Mandarin, to China, January 13, 1970) claims that Soviet deliveries to the government were temporarily interrupted in late 1939 and early 1940 because of armed incidents between the communists and government

is significant that when Mao Tse-tung was establishing his regime in Peking, the Soviet ambassador to China followed the Chiang Kai-shek government to Canton (unlike the American ambassador, Leighton Stuart, who remained for the time being in communist-occupied Nanking) and there negotiated with the National government for Soviet privileges in the border province of Sinkiang.

Once the communist regime was proclaimed on October 1, 1949, however, Moscow moved rapidly to establish an alliance with Peking. Mao Tse-tung went to Moscow to negotiate a series of agreements, signed on February 14, 1950, in which the Soviet Union relinquished many of its special privileges in China. The alliance presumably reflected the lessons the Soviets had learned from Tito's defection, for the Sino-Soviet treaty was more generous to China than any of the treaties Moscow negotiated with its Eastern European satellites.[3] Nevertheless, the Soviets retained some

---

forces; deliveries to Chungking were later resumed. Moscow has claimed no direct assistance to the Chinese communists until after the Japanese surrender in Manchuria in 1945 (see the twenty-eighth broadcast in the series cited above, Radio Moscow, in Mandarin, to China, February 4, 1970). See also S. Tikhvinskiy, "Geopolitical Fortunetelling," *Pravda*, February 15, 1970.

[3] Text of treaty in Raymond L. Garthoff (ed.), *Sino-Soviet Military Relations* (New York: Frederick A. Praeger, Inc., 1966), appendix B. Alone among Soviet bloc treaties negotiated during the period, the Sino-Soviet treaty specified that it was to be carried out "in conformity with the principles of equality, mutual benefit, mutual respect for national sovereignty and territorial integrity, and noninterference in internal affairs"— principles that with the addition of "mutual coexistence" were

special privileges (e.g., the Port Arthur Naval Base) and gained some others (e.g., certain "joint stock" companies, including one formed to exploit uranium and other ores in Sinkiang). These privileges were not relinquished until October 1954, after Stalin's death, when insistence upon these privileges was cited as one of the mistakes of his era.[4]

Soviet assistance to Peking in the development of an advanced strategic weapons system dates from an agreement signed in October 1954, by which Peking was singled out to receive a large-scale nuclear reactor and other aid that was not given to the East European satellites participating in the program of scientific and technical cooperation. Early research and training efforts were climaxed in October 1957 when Moscow agreed to help directly in the development of a nuclear weapons system, including, Peking has stated, the promise of a "sample" bomb. Such Soviet assistance had no parallel elsewhere in the bloc, and it stood in sharp contrast to the Soviet espousal, dating from the same period, of nonproliferation.[5]

One can speculate that from the outset the Soviet

---

to become Peking's famous "Five Principles of Peaceful Coexistence."

[4] See *The Anti-Stalin Campaign and International Communism* (New York: Columbia University Press, 1956).

[5] See Helmut Sonnenfeldt, "The Chinese Factor in Soviet Disarmament Policy," *China Quarterly*, April-June 1966; Walter C. Clemens, Jr., "A 'Most Puzzling Aspect' of Sino-Soviet Relations," *The Arms Race and Sino-Soviet Relations* (Stanford, Cal.: The Hoover Institution on War, Revolution, and Peace, 1968); and Alice Langley Hsieh, *Communist China's Strategy in the Nuclear Era* (Englewood Cliffs, N.J.: Prentice-Hall, 1962), p. 20.

leaders had qualms about the concessions that were needed to establish a partnership with Peking, and particularly about the unpredictable elements that were being introduced into bloc relations. Insofar as advanced weapons were concerned, assistance was being given to Peking to develop independent capabilities, despite the obvious Soviet preference for a monopoly within the bloc of advanced weapons, which would be utilized as it would determine in behalf of all members of the bloc.[6]

Despite Peking's special status within the bloc, by the late 1950s it became apparent that Moscow was unable to prevent a split in the alliance, which was to become even more serious than was the defection of Tito a decade earlier. The collapse of the Sino-Soviet alliance was all the more traumatic for the Soviets because of the size, population, and ideological appeal of Communist China, because of complex border problems between the two, and because of Peking's rapidly developing nuclear program.

Since the split, two major strategic considerations appear to have figured in Moscow's appraisal of its dispute with China: frontier security and nuclear strategy. Calculations of frontier security are complicated

[6] See Chapter 3, "Nuclear Proliferation and Soviet Arms Control Policy." The Soviet espousal during the late 1950s of proposals for a Pacific nuclear free zone, while aimed principally at the U.S. military presence in Asia, probably also reflected Moscow's genuine doubts regarding the wisdom of assisting a Chinese communist weapons program—hence, Peking's noticeably lukewarm and qualified concurrence in the Soviet position. A similar Sino-Soviet divergence became apparent in 1958 when Moscow announced a temporary halt in nuclear testing. See Hsieh, *Communist China's Strategy*, pp. 103–9.

by the fact that much of the Sino-Soviet border area is inhabited by Mongol and Turkic people who are ethnically and by political loyalty neither Chinese nor Russian. Before 1950 Moscow had sought to ensure frontier security in some sectors by stimulating separatist and "autonomy" movements in Sinkiang and Inner Mongolia; after the split, Moscow again tried to exploit minority nationalism in those areas. This effort was facilitated by the fact that the Maoist Cultural Revolution of the late 1960s particularly affected the Mongols and Uighurs of Inner Mongolia and Sinkiang in the purge of key local leaders and in the imposition of a rigorous sinification policy. Soviet political efforts were supplemented by more conventional reinforcements of border defenses. Inevitably, border incidents occurred, climaxed by the frontier clashes in Manchuria and Sinkiang during 1969. During this time the Sino-Soviet propaganda war became more intense. The early, veiled polemics about "great nation chauvinism" and minority policy and the exhortations for "vigilance" against unnamed enemies along the border gave way to open accusations that the other was making war preparations. Kosygin's visit to Peking in September 1969, after Ho Chi Minh's funeral, and the protracted border negotiations initiated in Peking in October 1969 only incompletely and temporarily muted those charges.[7]

[7] For some of the earlier examples, see Chou En-lai's 1968 charge that the Soviets were provocatively stationing "massive troops" along the Soviet-Chinese and Mongolian-Chinese borders and that Soviet planes "frequently" violated Chinese airspace (remarks at an Albanian reception in Peking, September 29, 1968). There were various reports of similar reinforcements on the Chinese side of the border, in part carried out under a

The second strategic consideration in the Sino-Soviet dispute involves broader problems of nuclear strategy. After "sputnik," Mao Tse-tung concluded that Soviet space and missile achievements had given the bloc a military and psychological momentum ("the East wind prevails over the West wind") that should be exploited.[8] The Soviet leaders were more cautious, however, and would not agree in 1958 to give Mao blanket assurances of nuclear support in his off-shore-island adventures. In June 1959 they withdrew Soviet assistance to Communist China's nuclear weapons program; and in 1960 they terminated all technical assistance, much of it of military significance. The subsequent Soviet announcement of its willingness to enter into a test ban agreement with the United States, on the eve of Peking's first nuclear test, gave rise to the extensive Sino-Soviet polemic of 1963 and, in effect, publicly buried the alliance.[9] In 1958 Moscow's concern was

---

directive from Lin Piao said to have been issued in July 1968. See Huhehot (Inner Mongolia) broadcast of November 17, 1968. For an unclassified report on the military situation along the border, see *Fei Ch'ing Yen-chiu* (Studies on Chinese Communism) (Taipei), vol. II, no. 11 (November 1968). The Manchurian incidents were reported in the Soviet, Chinese, and western press, in March and July 1969; those in Sinkiang, in May, June, and August 1969. For the Kosygin visit, see *New York Times*, September 12 and 25, 1969. For the Sino-Soviet border negotiations, see the Statement of the Government of the People's Republic of China, October 7, 1969, in *Peking Review*, no. 41 (October 10, 1969), the Communiqué announcing that the talks would begin October 20, 1969 (Peking, New China News Agency, October 18, 1969), and subsequent western press reports.

[8] See Zagoria, "The Maoist Assessment: The East Wind Prevails," *The Sino-Soviet Conflict*, pp. 160ff.

[9] This sequence of events was debated extensively between

that the Soviet Union might somehow be drawn unintentionally into a confrontation with the United States over Chinese actions. Soviet concern has since probably been expanded to encompass also the possibility, however remote, of a direct nuclear confrontation between the erstwhile socialist allies.

Moscow at first hesitated to boast openly of its nuclear superiority over China, but this inhibition began to disappear after the 1969 Ussuri incidents. In rebutting Peking's many statements that the "new Tsars" in Moscow are "paper tigers," Moscow's "unofficial" Radio Peace and Progress pointedly cited the Soviet arsenal of nuclear rockets and Peking's present lack of such weapons. Such commentaries since then have become quite routine; a recent Soviet broadcast, for example, argued that Mao Tse-tung's theory of "protracted war" is inapplicable in modern warfare in which the opponent has an arsenal of nuclear weapons and missiles.[10]

Currently, the China factor probably operates in two areas of Soviet policies related to arms control. Awareness of a threat from China probably intensifies the desire of Soviet leaders to resolve major world problems of nuclear strategy within the relatively manageable patterns of confrontation between the two

Peking and Moscow in 1963; English translations of the pertinent documents are given in William E. Griffith, *The Sino-Soviet Rift* (Cambridge, Mass.: MIT Press, 1964), section III.

[10] The Radio Peace and Progress broadcast (March 15, 1969) was reported in *New York Times*, March 21, 1969; the commentary on "protracted war" was broadcast by Radio Moscow, in Mandarin, to China, January 13, 1970, as part of a series of similar articles from a variety of Soviet sources. Moscow at first denied any intent at nuclear intimidation, but the broadcasts have become increasingly explicit nonetheless.

superpowers. The shock to Moscow of the breakdown of the Stalinist system of two opposing power blocs, highlighted more by Peking's defection than by any other factor, probably makes Moscow more anxious to resolve world problems on a bipolar basis in a context of arms control and mutual deterrence worked out with the United States.

At the same time, it is difficult to conceive of a way in which arms control agreements with the United States will ease the practical problems of Soviet relations with Peking, except for such incidental effects as releasing Soviet military and economic resources for Far Eastern border defenses. Certain types of arms control measures (e.g., the "hot line") conceivably lessen the risk of inadvertent Soviet involvement with the United States in a conflict originated by Peking, but that risk is in any case not great considering the moribund state of the Sino-Soviet alliance.

Moscow's dilemma is compounded by the fact that not only will arms control have little predictable effect on its immediate problems with China, but in the longer run, as China's nuclear and missile capabilities increase it could become very much a destabilizing factor in Soviet-American relations, for example, by engendering fears by either side that the other might be "colluding" with Peking. A notoriously unpredictable Chinese communist regime that is equally hostile toward the United States and the Soviet Union raises the nightmare possibility that it may one day give its support to one side or the other, thereby thoroughly upsetting whatever balance of strategic forces exists. Nevertheless, despite their apparent insolubility, Moscow's problems with Peking probably have worked to create an atmosphere that weighs on the side of

Soviet willingness to negotiate with the United States in an attempt to stabilize the nuclear confrontation.

## THE FUTURE OF SINO-SOVIET RELATIONS

The influence of the China factor on Soviet arms control policies will be determined in part by how Sino-Soviet relations develop, particularly after Mao's death and—even more important in view of the "lead time" required for both weapons development and arms control agreements—by how Soviet planners now subjectively view the future.

Communist China will go through an exceedingly difficult period during the early 1970s. The Communist Party has been wrecked as a unifying civilian element, and its reconstruction will not be easy. The cumulative economic and social-political impact of years of disruption is being felt in agriculture, industry, education, public discipline, and possibly also in the armed forces. The normal shortage of technical skills in China could become critical because the schools have not been able to operate properly for several years. The customary vulnerability of Chinese agriculture to the vagaries of weather has been heightened by several years of organizational neglect and disruption. There may be Chinese communist leaders who believe that under such stringent circumstances the dispute with the Soviet Union is a senseless dissipation of Chinese energies and an alienation of a potential source of assistance. With a critical situation at home, these leaders may also see the restoration of the Sino-Soviet alliance as a deterrent to possible attempts by the United States or Taiwan to exploit the situation in China militarily.

Such reasoning is likely to apply particularly to

younger, professional military men whose concerns may be more with the technical equipment of the armed forces than with political matters. Economic development technicians may be somewhat less persuaded of the usefulness, in economic terms, of restoring the Sino-Soviet alliance because nonstrategic items can probably be procured from the free world on generally better terms than from the Soviet bloc. Both military and economic specialists will remember that, despite impressive Soviet technical and other assistance in the early years of Communist China's economic development and military modernization, economic assistance was tapered off even before the Sino-Soviet split, with loan repayments exceeding aid deliveries during the later years. Even if the alliance were restored, military specialists would not expect to receive significant Soviet assistance in the development of advanced weapons systems. Probably the most useful economic benefits to be expected would be a market for certain Chinese exports that are not easily marketable in the West, and possibly long-term credits —though the history of limited Soviet credits to China would not make Chinese officials unduly optimistic in this regard. On the strategic side, China's planners probably would welcome the restoration of the deterrent aspects of the Sino-Soviet alliance, bearing in mind, however, the ambiguous Soviet position at the time of the 1958 offshore-islands crisis.

Whatever limited economic and strategic advantages might accrue from the termination of the Sino-Soviet split, the Chinese leaders must consider the political advantage of China's present posture. Mao and his potential successors probably recognize the nationalistic and unifying role for China of the dispute with the Soviet Union, which could well be the most widely popular aspect of Maoism in its current phase. Even the Chinese on Taiwan grudgingly concede their admiration for the way the Chinese communists have reasserted their position against the Russians. Hostility toward Russia does not have to be stimulated artificially like the "hate America" sentiment. If Peking, in times of trouble, needs the image of an external foe, the Soviet Union is much more suited to the role than the United States.

On balance, it is unlikely that even a more moderate successor to Mao will be willing to make the ideological and policy concessions that would be required to restore the Sino-Soviet alliance; it is more likely that a degree of hostility toward the Soviet Union will be maintained as a politically useful unifying element. If there is an outbreak of severe factionalism in Peking at the time of Mao's death, conceivably one group or another might seek Soviet support, but it is more likely that various factions will vie with one another in their "patriotic" and "revolutionary" Chinese fervor to maintain the Maoist opposition to Soviet revisionism.[11]

On the Soviet side, it is possible that some leaders

[11] Charges that some Chinese communist leaders who were purged in the course of the Cultural Revolution sought to "collude" with Moscow are probably highly oversimplified. It is doubtful that any likely Chinese communist leadership that might come to power would be able or willing to effect a genuine reconciliation with Moscow. It is interesting that only one Chinese communist official of note has surfaced as a defector to Moscow—Shen Shao-yu (Wang Ming). Shen's case is hardly typical, since he has been held up as an example of deviation from Maoism since the 1930s when he served in Moscow as the Chinese Communist Party's representative to the Comintern. Shen survived after returning to China presumably because of his value

may be more sanguine about restoring Sino-Soviet friendship because they have a higher estimate of the effectiveness of Moscow's ideological leadership in the communist movement and of the value of Soviet assistance and security guarantees. They may also underestimate the historical, popular Chinese antipathy toward Russia.[12] Balanced against any possible Soviet optimism, which may focus on the time of Mao's death or perhaps on a further disintegration of centralized control in China, is the professional caution of Soviet bureaucrats and military men, particularly when they make estimates involving long-range strategic problems. It seems likely that Soviet planners, even while awaiting a possibly more favorable turn of events, do not *count* on improvements in relations with China and that they do not exclude hostilities with China in their strategic planning.

A relatively cautious Soviet policy may serve to maintain points of friction or Chinese resentment. The

---

as a "negative example." He recently emerged as a propagandist and pamphleteer in Moscow where, according to Peking, he fled on the pretext of seeking medical treatment. See "China—Cultural Revolution or Counter-Revolutionary Coup," published March 19, 1969, by the Communist Party of Canada in the party journal, *Canadian Tribune*, and subsequently by the Novosti Press Agency Publishing House (Moscow, n.d.). See also "History Sentenced the Wang Ming Renegade Clique to Death," broadcast by the Chinese Communist Huhehot (Inner Mongolia) radio June 17, 1969.

[12] Soviet analyses ascribing recent Chinese developments to "Mao and his clique" might seem to imply that Moscow expects a more favorable trend in China following Mao's death. Other Soviet statements, however, have attempted a historical-sociological explanation of Maoism that could be read to mean that Maoism may survive Mao. See, for example, the editorial

Soviets, for example, are not likely again to rely on the Sino-Soviet alliance in place of "traditional," conservative border politics—which are likely to give rise to various clashes—nor are they, even during a period of relative thaw when some economic or even military assistance might be given to Peking, likely again to include in that assistance technical help in developing advanced weapons systems or to offer blanket security guarantees, thus excluding the type of assistance that would be most persuasive to Peking.

The likely predominant Soviet attitude toward Peking during the 1970s will be a desire to retain as much control as possible over variable factors, and to avoid giving Peking the latitude it once enjoyed as a Soviet ally. This attitude itself will make re-establishment of genuinely cordial relations unlikely.[13]

In summary, it is highly unlikely that the Sino-Soviet alliance can be restored within the next decade or so to the effective working relationship that it was during the early 1950s. At the same time, an outbreak of full-scale hostilities also appears unlikely, given the caution of both sides in such matters. Within these ex-

---

carried in the April 13, 1968, issue of the Soviet periodical *Kommunist*.

[13] That Moscow is relatively reconciled to the split with Peking is suggested also by Soviet efforts, unsuccessful so far, to obtain endorsement of its position or condemnation of Peking from the world communist movement. Brezhnev's report to the June 1969 meeting of Communist and Workers' Parties in Moscow included a lengthy denunciation of Peking, and yet the final report of that conference failed altogether to mention the China problem. See Brezhnev's speech reported by TASS on June 7, 1969, and the "Main Document" adopted by the conference, reported by TASS on June 10, 1969.

tremes, one can expect wide fluctuations. There are likely to be repeated periods of tension and outbreaks of border incidents; even a rupture of state-to-state relations is possible, perhaps after a particularly serious border incident.[14] On the other hand, after Mao's death, there may be mutual efforts to restore some surface cordiality and perhaps, particularly for western consumption, even the appearance of an alliance. During such times of minimal tension, Peking might receive some limited Soviet assistance. However, it is very doubtful that a "Sino-Soviet bloc" will ever again exist in fact.

## STRATEGIC IMPLICATIONS

The fact that Communist China is a nuclear nation and that it could by 1975 have a modest strategic delivery capability is an obviously important factor in the arms control policy of any nation that faces a potential threat from Peking.[15] For the Soviet Union, the strategic problem in regard to a nuclear China has four principal aspects.

[14] The March 1969 Ussuri and subsequent incidents are instructive in this regard, in that both sides were careful not to permit military action to exceed an "acceptable" level, even while propagandists were given a free rein in exchanging very serious charges. At the time of this writing, the charges continue but so do diplomatic efforts to keep border tension within manageable limits. See footnote 7 above.

[15] See statement of Secretary of Defense Melvin R. Laird, U.S., Congress, Senate, Joint Session of the Armed Services Committee and the Subcommittee on Department of Defense Appropriations, *Fiscal Year 1971 Defense Program and Budget* (Washington, D.C.: U.S. Government Printing Office, February 20, 1970),

First is Moscow's concern that it will be able to deter or repel any strategic attack from China. On balance, the Soviets probably feel that, with their nuclear superiority over China, they can deter such an attack, even given the "reckless" view of nuclear warfare attributed to Mao by Soviet propaganda. There has been no public discussion in the Soviet Union of a "China-directed" ABM system, thin or otherwise, but it seems likely that Soviet planners may want to supplement their deterrent capability with a China-oriented anti-missile system.[16] The implications for arms control are clear: Moscow would not likely agree to arms limitations that restrict its freedom to deploy a missile defense system against China or that appear to downgrade the Soviet deterrent posture against China.[17]

---

pp. 107–9. Secretary Laird estimates that by the mid-1970s Peking could have 80–100 operational MRBMs and possibly 10–25 ICBMs, if certain production problems are solved.

[16] Peking has claimed in its propaganda that Moscow has plans for an anti-Chinese ABM system parallel to U.S. plans, but this accusation may reflect nothing more than Peking's line of charging Soviet-American "collusion" in every conceivable context. See Peking broadcast of March 1, 1969. See also, however, President Richard Nixon's press conference of March 14, 1969, in which he stated that Soviet ABM radars are now being directed also against China.

[17] A satisfactory deterrent against China may, in the Soviet view, require a Soviet nuclear preponderance great enough that even after a nuclear exchange with the United States sufficient strength remains to constitute a plausible threat against China. The lack of such a preponderance might play into the hands of those Peking strategists who count on a Soviet-American nuclear war to degrade the China deterrent of those countries. See Harry G. Gelber, "The Impact of Chinese ICBM's on Strategic Deterrence," *Orbis*, vol. XIII, no. 2 (May 1969).

A second aspect of the Soviet strategic problem relates to border defenses. The fact that China and the Soviet Union share the world's longest land border—inhabited on both sides by sensitive Mongol, Turkic, and other minorities—has historically been the most prominent factor in Soviet (and tsarist) policy toward China. Moscow's, at times, heavy-handed efforts to supplement conventional border defenses by establishing special privileges and a buffer zone of friendly or at least neutral states or warlords in Sinkiang, Outer and Inner Mongolia, and Manchuria, were an early irritant in Sino-Soviet relations. In the course of the Sino-Soviet dispute, as noted above, border problems again arose. A new addition to the dispute was Chinese irredentism, which raised an issue of particular sensitivity for Moscow. At a time when Moscow was berating Mao for his tolerance of the "imperialist" enclaves of Hong Kong and Macao, Mao pointedly noted the much greater territory seized from China by Russia in various treaty settlements of the past century, involving large areas in Soviet Central Asia and the Soviet Far East. Also, Peking is far from reconciled to the separation from China of Outer Mongolia; there have been charges in the Ulan Bator and Moscow presses of Chinese "chauvinist" ambitions in this area. These accusations and counteraccusations between Peking and Moscow are probably not without substance.[18]

While the Soviets probably do not rule out the development of large-scale border hostilities, they prob-

[18] See footnote 7 above. See also the article on Chinese ambitions in Outer Mongolia, *Izvestiia*, January 7, 1968; and William E. Griffith, "Sino-Soviet Relations 1964–65," *China Quarterly* (January–March 1966).

ably also do not expect a concerted effort by Peking to reconquer the territory controlled by earlier Chinese dynasties.[19] Militating against a major Chinese-initiated border war (as distinct from various incursions and incidents) are the remoteness of most of the Sino-Soviet border from Chinese logistic centers and the inadequate and vulnerable rail network to the border; the general logistic weakness in long-range operations of the Chinese forces; severe shortages of many kinds of modern equipment; and the vulnerability to retaliatory air attack of some of China's principal industrial complexes in Inner Mongolia and Manchuria.

The Soviet Union probably views the problem of border defenses as primarily a tactical one, requiring for the foreseeable future continuing heavy deployments of conventional forces supplemented by air defense and possibly short-range and medium-range missiles. So far as arms control agreements are concerned, the Soviets will not want to curtail the military manpower required for border defenses nor to foreclose the option of a tactical use of nuclear weapons should conventional forces be unable to deal with a Chinese border incursion.

Concern for its border security, thus, is not likely to

[19] In this connection, it is significant that at the time of the March 2, 1969, Ussuri incident, Peking made clear that the dispute involved the question of whether Chen-pao (Damanskiy) island lies within Chinese territory as defined in the treaty of November 14, 1860. Peking has consistently said it was willing to take various Russian-Chinese treaties as the "basis" for border negotiations, even though it wanted the "unequal" and therefore invalid nature of these treaties recognized. See Peking Foreign Ministry statement of March 12, 1969, reprinted in *New York Times*, March 12, 1969.

affect greatly Moscow's policy toward presently fore-seeable arms control negotiations, since these do not in-volve restrictions on conventional or tactical forces and arms.[20] In fact, as suggested earlier, curtailment of the strategic arms race could conceivably ease the Soviet border-defense problem by releasing for con-ventional and tactical use some of the funds now ear-marked for strategic weapons systems.

A third aspect of the Soviet strategic view of China is the question of possible Soviet intervention in Peking or in outlying sections of China to support a situation that holds promise of making China, or a part of it, more amenable to Soviet aims than it is under the leadership of Mao Tse-tung. It is hard to imagine that Moscow has not given thought to the contingency of a province, a faction, or a clique splitting with the Mao leadership and appealing for Soviet help. The Soviet invasion of Czechoslovakia illustrates the fact that Moscow does not consider its relations with neighboring communist regimes as a purely political problem; it underscores also the costs and risks Moscow is willing to assume in order to safeguard its interests in neighboring countries.[21] Soviet military planners

[20] The coincidence in timing between the border talks initiated in Peking in October 1969 and the preliminary strategic arms limitation talks begun in Helsinski in November 1969 has sug-gested a relationship between the two to some observers. This is difficult to establish, however. For Peking's predictable reac-tion to SALT, see *Peking Review*, no. 46 (November 14, 1969), p. 28.

[21] Peking's condemnation of the Warsaw Pact invasion of Czechoslovakia was largely exploitation of a propaganda wind-fall, but it also reflected real concern that the Czech invasion might constitute a precedent for Soviet military intervention in

undoubtedly recognize that even in an outlying province of China military intervention would be a formidable undertaking and more complicated than past such undertakings (e.g., in Sinkiang) that went almost unnoticed in the outside world. However, the Soviets almost certainly would not be interested in an international agreement that would limit their flexibility to intervene in China if a seemingly profitable contingency should develop. The problem again is somewhat marginal to arms control problems because the Soviet military capability required for intervention in China presumably would be principally conventional and tactical, rather than strategic.

A special case would arise in the event that an outside power became involved in military action against the China mainland. Soviet and Chinese commentators, if they have referred to the Sino-Soviet alliance at all in recent years, have suggested that the alliance is virtually moribund.[22] Nevertheless, Moscow might seize the opportunity of Chinese involvement in hostilities to force a political reorientation in Peking as the price for Soviet

---

a remote part of China, such as Sinkiang Province, where Soviet military intervention has occurred in the past. See the Sinkiang People's Broadcasting Station broadcast of September 8, 1968, quoted in *China News Analysis* (Hong Kong), no. 730 (October 25, 1968).

[22] See, for example, the Soviet journal *International Affairs* for October 1967, which notes of the 1950 Sino-Soviet treaty that "the Chinese leaders' present policy has largely deprived it of its meaning." The same journal, in the issue for February 1968, states that the treaty "was one of the major guarantees of China's national security," but Maoist policies have "considerably weakened China's international position and isolated it from the forces of socialism."

military assistance. Observers in Taiwan have sometimes speculated that the Soviets would not intervene
against a Chinese Nationalist landing south of the
Yangtze, except possibly to establish a more responsive
regime in the north under the guise of "assistance."
Such intervention also would presumably not require
strategic nuclear weapons.

The fourth aspect of the Soviet strategic problem
relates to fears of being drawn into major hostilities
initiated by Peking over some issue of secondary importance to Moscow. Moscow's sensitivity in this regard was illustrated during the 1958 offshore-islands
crisis, when Moscow would not issue a nuclear guarantee
for Peking until it was already clear that the crisis would
abate. While the present danger of Moscow's becoming
involved in hostilities in behalf of Peking might appear
slim, Peking's presence does complicate Moscow's maneuvering in such limited-war situations as Vietnam.
Arms control measures and a general trend toward détente might be viewed by Moscow as a means of reduc-
ing even further the danger of "catalytic" war in the
Far East.

## IDEOLOGICAL IMPLICATIONS

The Sino-Soviet dispute has had from the outset a
heavy ideological content, involving arguments over
such questions as the continuation of the class struggle
even after the establishment of a communist regime, the
form the transition from socialism to communism should
take, the nature of the conflict between socialist and
"imperialist" countries, the inevitability or noninevita-
bility of major war, and the possibility of a communist

seizure of power by means other than "armed struggle."
Soviet disarmament tactics have figured importantly in
this ideological debate, and, in fact, the most extensive
Sino-Soviet polemic was set off by the Soviet signing of
the partial Nuclear Test Ban Treaty in 1963.[23] In entering into that treaty, Moscow simply ignored the expected
Chinese ideological argument, which was left to professional polemicists for rebuttal, and there is no indication that since that time Moscow's arms control and
disarmament policies have been significantly affected by
Peking's ideological position.[24] As Peking moved into
more extreme phases of the Cultural Revolution, its
anti-Soviet propaganda became more and more strident
and, ideologically perhaps, less persuasive; Moscow, on
the other hand, began to engage in "scholarly" Marxist-
Leninist analyses of Chinese phenomena, in the course
of which it virtually ceased to take Maoism seriously,
even as a deviant of Marxism-Leninism.

The aspects of Peking's argument that are relevant to
the question of arms control can be summarized as fol-
lows: (1) in war, men are more important than weapons, and political-ideological factors more decisive than
technology (this is Mao Tse-tung's "guerrilla" concept
of modern war) ; (2) as an aspirant to great-power
status in the world, China, nevertheless, will not be

[23] See Clemens, "World Views in Conflict," *The Arms Race
and Sino-Soviet Relations*, and the documents cited in footnote
9 above.

[24] There is evidence that Soviet disarmament conference tactics
were influenced at various times by considerations of the relationship with Peking, but since 1962 or 1963 the Soviet negotiating
position has largely disregarded the interests and protests of Peking. See Sonnenfeldt, "The Chinese Factor in Soviet Disarmament Policy."

denied the technological appurtenances of such status —including nuclear weapons and missiles; (3) except as a temporary tactical expedient in a "protracted struggle," accommodation with the "enemy" is tantamount to surrender; and (4) any tactical or strategic advantage must be followed up aggressively either politically or militarily. As corollaries to these points, Peking argues that Soviet advocacy of arms control and Soviet willingness to negotiate with the United States represent surrender to U.S. nuclear blackmail. Mao Tse-tung maintained with particular emotion that the communist countries must not express any fear of nuclear war, lest such fear lead to a relaxation of the struggle against the West. The Soviets, claiming a more sophisticated understanding of modern weaponry, rebut the Chinese points by stressing the destructiveness of nuclear war,[25] the relative insignificance of minor weapons superiority by one side or the other in view of the destructive capability of both sides, and the possibility of pursuing communist bloc aims by means short of war.

Much of the debate is misleading. In the discussion of what percent of the world's population might be killed in a nuclear war, for example, the fact has become obscured that Peking no more than Moscow wishes to initiate a nuclear holocaust. Peking is more reckless than Moscow in the polemic, but in its policies it actually has exercised great caution, for example, refraining from any significant hostile actions against the Chinese Nationalist-held offshore islands throughout the Kennedy-Johnson years. The most dangerous crisis of that period, the Cuban missile confrontation, was Soviet initiated

[25] See footnote 10 above.

and subsequently described by Peking as reckless "adventurism" (followed by shameful "capitulationism"). The polemic cannot be taken at face value, and many of the charges and countercharges are distortions. The sharp dispute, however, does reveal Peking's claim to be the spokesman for revolutionary forces in Asia and the underdeveloped world and its belief that as a relative "have not" nation it can only lose in a stabilization of the East-West balance of power.

Peking in recent times has carried Mao's dictum that "political power grows out of the barrel of a gun" to ludicrous extremes, in sharp contrast to the periods when Chou En-lai skillfully manipulated communist "united front" and "peaceful coexistence" tactics. Nevertheless, throughout his career Mao has emphasized armed struggle and violence as the principal form of revolution. Chou En-lai's negotiating skill has been used by Mao to neutralize the opposition or to maneuver the Chinese communists into a more advantageous position for a new assault by armed force, to gain allies for such a struggle, or to obtain a respite during periods of adversity. But the negotiated settlement has never been considered an end in itself. In the present era of East-West struggle, whether in the context of Vietnam negotiations, arms control talks, or Peking's discussions with the United States at Warsaw, the Chinese stress essentially the same point—that the communists must not yield in negotiations any position that will be advantageous in the struggle to come, and that negotiations and the desire for peace must not be permitted to sap the communist determination to fight.[26]

[26] Peking late last year republished a speech made by Mao Tse-tung on March 5, 1949, at a time when negotiations with

The effectiveness of Peking's argument derives in part from the fact that its tenets are consistent with Marxist-Leninist dogma; Moscow could reply only with the ideologically doubtful but otherwise very telling point that Mao Tse-tung did not understand the awesome destructiveness of modern nuclear weapons. It is in fact likely that Mao did understand the effectiveness of nuclear weapons, and that he therefore was almost as anxious as the Soviet leaders to avoid nuclear war. Convinced also of the power of politics, however, Mao hoped, by denying any fear of nuclear weapons, to play upon the West's reluctance to utilize its nuclear advantage.

Whatever may have been the ideological merits, from a Marxist-Leninist viewpoint, of Peking's position in the dispute, recent Chinese polemic has lost much of its effectiveness because of its strident, almost paranoid emphasis on Soviet-American "collusion" in the "encirclement" of Communist China. One article issued by the official Peking news agency charged that the United States and the Soviet Union had formed a "counterrevolutionary alliance against China" and had manipulated various countries into accepting the Nonproliferation Treaty under which nonnuclear countries will be "controlled and subjugated" protectorates of Washington and of the "new Tsars" in Moscow.[27]

---

the Nanking government were being contemplated. The article includes an excellent explanation of Mao's view of the role of negotiations in an over-all struggle. See "Report to the Second Plenary Session of the Seventh Central Committee of the Communist Party of China," reprinted in *Peking Review*, November 29, 1969.

[27] New China News Agency, International Service, March 9, 1969.

Moscow's decision in 1963 to proceed with the nuclear test ban agreement despite the expected polemics from Peking indicated the extent to which it is possible for Moscow to ignore or bypass ideological arguments. With the increasing belligerence of the propaganda battle between Peking and Moscow (especially after the 1969 Ussuri River border incidents), it will presumably be even easier for Moscow to proceed according to its own interests rather than according to any particular ideological prescription. In fact, as the Chinese Cultural Revolution moved into more and more extreme phases, Moscow's ideological rebuttals became by comparison increasingly persuasive. However, in the longer run the most telling fact is likely to be the nonideological point that Moscow finds a balance between the superpowers acceptable as a basis for further competition, while Peking, painfully conscious of its inferiority, considers intolerable any stabilization of the status quo no matter what the rationale. Expressed in ideological terms, Peking ideologists appear to be more dogmatic, leftist, and doctrinaire Marxist-Leninists than those in Moscow. At a time when Moscow may be trying to enhance its "peaceful" and "responsible" image—even at the cost of its "revolutionary" image—such an impression may be quite acceptable to Moscow.

## Relations with Noncommunist Countries

In the informal division of labor between Peking and Moscow before the Sino-Soviet split, the Chinese experience was proclaimed by Peking to be relevant particularly to underdeveloped countries. The history of Chinese communism provided a great range of lessons, from guerrilla warfare to techniques of economic development, that were said to be applicable to newly independent countries and to those still under colonial rule. After the Sino-Soviet split, Peking competed openly with Moscow for influence in all countries, but in practice and theory it continued to emphasize its special role in the underdeveloped countries in Asia, Africa, and Latin America. As Lin Piao said, the "cities" of the world, i.e., the developed countries, which according to Marx should be nearest to revolution, for the moment are not quite so ready to accept the "thought" of Mao Tse-tung as the underdeveloped "countryside."[28] At the same time, Peking propagandists have lost no opportunity to proclaim Mao's influence on radical and other groups in the United States and other western countries, including Negroes and rioting students.

Specific Chinese communist courses of action in third countries have taken many forms in the past few years, including overt military action (India), encouragement and assistance to revolutionary movements (Indonesia, India, Burma, Thailand, Malaysia, the Philippines, and so on), and various forms of assistance to established non-communist governments that were susceptible to Chinese influence because of their radical orientation or other special factors [Mali, Guinea, Ghana, Congo (Brazzaville], Pakistan, Cambodia, and so on). In almost every instance, Chinese communist actions in effect constituted a challenge to the Soviet Union, which for its part reacted by increasingly emphasizing conventional diplomatic and economic tactics, including Brezhnev's so far un-

[28] "Long Live the Victory of People's War," English translation in *Peking Review*, September 3, 1965.

defined call of June 7, 1969, for an Asian regional security arrangement.[29]

The Sino-Soviet competition for influence in these countries is an important aspect of the Sino-Soviet clash, but with certain exceptions it is not directly relevant to the problem of arms control. For example, Peking's earlier successes and later setbacks in Africa have had no impact on arms control efforts, except the indirect one of influencing voting patterns in the United Nations to the advantage of Taipei.

There are, however, a few noncommunist countries whose position in the Sino-Soviet dispute has strategic and, therefore, arms control implications. Of these, the most crucial may be India and Japan, each of which has figured in the development of the dispute. India and Japan, countries with a potential nuclear capability, feel immediately threatened by Chinese nuclear developments and, therefore, require special consideration in regard to nonproliferation. The Chinese invasion of the Indian border territory was one of the most bitter issues in the Sino-Soviet dispute. Peking took the position that Soviet assistance to India was a betrayal of a fraternal socialist country, while Moscow claimed that Peking's adventurism on the border threatened to negate, for a barren mountain area, the influence in India that had been carefully nurtured by the bloc for over a decade.

Sino-Japanese relations have always been a sensitive political issue in both countries. For Japan, mainland China is both a tempting economic partner and a threatening, hostile, nuclear-equipped potential enemy. It was in relations with Japan that Peking in 1958 first mani-

[29] See Brezhnev's report to the international meeting of Communist and Workers' Parties, Moscow, June 7, 1969.

fested its current extremist, dogmatist foreign policy, following half a decade of seemingly successful "people's diplomacy." India and Japan, at opposite ends of China's periphery, obviously are important factors in the total Asian policy of both Moscow and Peking—including the arms control policies of both countries.

Peking currently is hostile and uncompromising toward both Japan and India, and Moscow is at this time ahead of Peking in the competition for influence in both countries (including a lead in influence within their communist movements) . However, both Peking's tactics and Moscow's lead are susceptible to outside developments (such as the Czech crisis, which obviously hurt Moscow in both countries) , and present trends are not necessarily immutable.

Indonesia is another interesting example of Sino-Soviet competition for influence. Prior to the abortive coup which led to Sukarno's downfall, Peking and Moscow were offering assistance to both the government and the communist movement of Indonesia; Peking far overreached itself in its backing of the unsuccessful coup and as a consequence lost all of its conventional and most of its revolutionary assets in Indonesia. Moscow's more conservative approach had greater flexibility and permitted it to salvage some assets and, after an interruption, even to resume aid to Indonesia. When Peking, prior to the coup failure, argued that nuclear proliferation not only was not to be feared but should, in the interest of world revolution and "peace," be encouraged, it is conceivable that the Chinese had in mind some form of nuclear assistance to Sukarno. Whether such thinking in Peking was ever very far advanced is problematical, but the coup may have taught Peking the same lesson about the uncertainties of world politics that Moscow learned from the Sino-Soviet split: there are definite risks involved even in nuclear proliferation to a friendly regime.[30] In any case, it is doubtful that China has the technological resources to give more than token nuclear assistance, which would not be effective unless the country in question already had substantial capabilities in the field of nuclear development.

Relations with third countries thus enter into Soviet arms control policies in three ways. First, the Soviets have used arms control advocacy and negotiations as a political instrument to gain influence in third countries, for example, by playing upon fears of nuclear warfare and upon neutralist and pacifist tendencies. Most Soviet arms control proposals in recent years have had a very heavy propaganda content of this type. Second, the Soviets are concerned about how to react to possible Chinese nuclear threats against third countries, either within or without the framework of safeguards created by the Nonproliferation Treaty and the United Nations. Third, the Soviets are also aware of the danger of Chinese proliferation of advanced weapons to third countries—a somewhat hypothetical threat at this time, but one that would nevertheless be difficult to counteract.

[30] The question of whether Peking might give its communist ally Albania token assistance in the field of missiles or nuclear weapons is a more difficult one. Albania is no conceivable threat to China but a considerable irritant to the Soviet Union. Like so many aspects of Moscow's China problem, this question also appears to lie outside the area in which arms control measures are likely to be effective.

## Appraisal of the China Factor

The Soviet Union has several objectives in regard to China which have a bearing on its arms control policies: to deter any attack from China against its territory; to maintain the security of its borders with China; to maintain a military capability for contingency use within China; to avoid being drawn into a major war with China or with the West over Chinese issues; to preserve its lead in competition with Peking for influence in noncommunist countries; to maintain (or repair) its ideological leadership among communist regimes and revolutionary movements; and to seize any opportunity for healing the schism in world communism on its terms.

These aims limit Soviet flexibility in arms control negotiations in certain specific regards. China, for the foreseeable future, will be hopelessly outclassed by the superpowers in strategic capability regardless of any likely U.S.-U.S.S.R. limitation on strategic delivery vehicles or warheads. Moscow will want to keep it this way. Furthermore, the Soviet Union—like the United States—may wish to retain the option of developing and deploying a missile defense system against China to guard against the failure of deterrence or to counteract possible Chinese nuclear blackmail. Despite formidable numbers, Chinese conventional forces suffer from a lack of modern equipment and a severe logistic handicap for operations beyond the Chinese border. Nevertheless, border-defense needs and force requirements for contingency use within China will limit Soviet flexibility in agreeing to any curtailment of conventional forces, even if Moscow retains—as it almost certainly will—the option of a tactical use of nuclear weapons if required to repel a Chinese border incursion.

The Soviet objective of avoiding war with the West over Chinese issues is facilitated by the moribund state of the Sino-Soviet alliance, by various arms control measures vis-à-vis the United States, and by such safeguards as the "hot line."

In the ideological sphere, arms control negotiations may undermine somewhat Soviet doctrinal purity, but whether Soviet influence and leadership are thereby in fact adversely affected is a complex and shifting question. The Soviets' espousal of arms control and disarmament measures, for example, may help them maintain their image of flexibility and "peacefulness," particularly among noncommunist and neutral states. At the same time, it could detract from their "revolutionary" image within the communist movement and, to that extent, play into Peking's hands. During recent years, the Soviets have apparently felt that the "peaceful" image is more important than the "revolutionary" one, and have therefore largely ignored Peking's ideological charges, particularly as they became more and more extreme. In the future, more crucial considerations bearing on its strategic relationship with the United States may override considerations of "image" and "ideology" altogether.

One caveat needs to be added to the foregoing. It is likely that Moscow's tolerance will reach its limit when Peking can begin to make a reasonably persuasive case that it is reaching parity with some aspect of the Soviet (and therefore American) advanced weapons capability. Regardless of any sophisticated appraisal of the over-all situation, Moscow would not want so to restrict its maneuverability in weapons systems development and deployment as to give Peking an opening to claim to have "outstripped" the Soviet Union in any aspect of nuclear or missile technology. The Soviet Union's sensitivity in the past to a "missile gap" between it and the United States is likely to be intensified at any suggestion that Peking is closing the gap between them.

The basically frustrating nature of the China problem for Moscow must be recognized. It is not susceptible to simple solution by maintenance of weapons superiority, deployment of border garrisons, or advocacy of non-proliferation. Nor can it be solved by conventional Marxist-Leninist means. To describe Maoism as "petty bourgeois nationalism" does not in fact reduce Moscow's ideological and strategic difficulties. As noted above, even patiently waiting for Mao's demise and for more "rational" leaders to assume power in Peking will not adequately ease Moscow's problems. Consequently, it is quite likely that relations with Peking may contribute to Moscow's hopes for a solution to certain strategic questions in a bipolar context of negotiations with the United States, even while recognizing that such negotiations cannot in any very direct way ease its difficulties with Peking.

# 5

## Soviet Policy Toward Europe

### INTRODUCTION

TWENTY YEARS AFTER THE founding of the North Atlantic Treaty Organization, "new looks" toward Europe are being taken in many quarters—not only by West Europeans and the Nixon administration but by the Kremlin and its putative allies. Will these new looks lead to an intensification of earlier trends toward détente, or to a consolidation of two armed and hostile camps facing one another in Central Europe? Will the European nations—western and eastern—work more closely with one another or will divisive tendencies become sharper? Will the presence of the superpowers be increased, reduced, or modified in important ways?

This chapter focuses on the likely course of Soviet policy toward Europe during the first half of the 1970s, with particular emphasis on the implications for arms control and strategic planning. The nature of Moscow's policy is but one of many interdependent variables, for it will shape and be shaped by a wide array of events and by the decisions of other actors. Given these uncertainties, flat predictions are impossible. What can be done, however, is to outline the alternative courses of action the Kremlin may consider pursuing, given different combinations of challenges and opportunities in the Soviets' domestic and international environments. The weakness of this approach to forecasting is its heavy attention to objective, deterministic considerations as opposed to the more subjective and voluntaristic factors in history. Even if the present Soviet leaders remain in power during the first half of the 1970s, their policy attitudes may change. *A fortiori*, new men with new ideas may come into power, persons whose responses to possible alternate environments may differ in crucial ways from those of their predecessors. The role of objective, relatively permanent operating factors, however, should not be minimized. Even if Messrs. Brezhnev and Kosygin and other leaders should be replaced, their successors will probably share many of their goals and will be constrained by similar dilemmas of power and responsibility.

We begin with a general survey of the attitudes of Soviet policy-makers toward Eastern Europe in the late 1960s, both prior to and since the invasion of Czechoslovakia. Following that, the changing place of Western Europe in the Kremlin's strategic calculations is examined. Given that context, the evolution of Soviet views on the requisites of European security and arms control is discussed, with particular attention to the short-term and long-term problems arising from West Germany's political, economic, and military potential. Finally, five major strategies which Moscow conceivably might consider during the early 1970s are assessed.

Of these options, the Kremlin may well be most inclined toward a conservative, status quo orientation. On the other hand, given the difficulties and dangers inherent in this and in other alternatives—an indirect advance, a forward strategy, and isolationism—Soviet leaders may come increasingly to perceive a fundamental utility in a strategy of interdependence premised on the mutual interests of the northern nations in nonantagonistic, cooperative solutions to common problems. Whether such an orientation can gain general acceptance in the next five—or even fifty—years will hinge on the development of many factors affecting western as well as Soviet and East European policymakers.

## Evolving Soviet Relations with Eastern Europe

The year 1968 may turn out to be a historic bench mark in Soviet policy, marking the ascendancy of an inward-looking, conservative orientation over the ebullient, confident outlook of the Khrushchev era. As the year began, the Kremlin leadership was confronted with a sense of drift in foreign affairs and by a rising tide of dissent and unrest within the country. The decision to attempt by force of arms to repress the liberalization of Czechoslovakia, epitomized Moscow's concern with regaining active control of events that seemed to be developing spontaneously and in directions contrary to Soviet preferences.

Khrushchev's successors had done little to halt the trend toward disintegration in Eastern Europe, which he had helped to initiate. The Kremlin's situation, in some important respects, was like Washington's in that both countries were encountering mounting difficulty in utilizing their superpower status to ensure conformity or even coordination in their alliance affairs. The blows to Soviet rule under Khrushchev's reign were many and cannot be minimized: acceptance of "separate roads" and "polycentrism" as practiced and preached by Tito and Togliatti; revolts in Poland and Hungary; open rifts with Albania and China; the need for a wall to halt East German emigration; the beginnings of an independent policy in Bucharest; great difficulties in organizing a "unity" conference against China. Problems of this nature have continued to face the Kremlin leadership since Khrushchev's removal, some of them becoming still more troublesome, in part because Bucharest and Prague attempted to avoid the kind of overt challenges that had provoked armed intervention against the Nagy regime in 1956. Rumania's autonomous course, though its most apparent origins dated from 1962, picked up momentum between 1964 and 1968 and included deviations not only on issues of economic integration but also on such political questions as the Arab-Israeli war, the Nonproliferation Treaty, and the value of the Dubcek reforms. Rumania was joined by other East European states (and some West European communist parties) in resisting Moscow's intermittent pleas for an international communist conference. And throughout Eastern Europe—not least of all in the German Democratic Republic—economic innovations proceeded apace, with political consequences that could only be guessed.

The aftermath, as well as the origins, of the Soviet-sponsored intervention in Czechoslovakia witnessed a much-intensified Soviet emphasis on monolithic conformity within the bloc. The invasion of Czechoslovakia reflected a new determination to hold fast, to preserve the line against encroachments from the outside or innovation from within. A warning had been signaled that Moscow would be less lenient toward autonomous policies, such as those that had been followed by Rumania and Czechoslovakia.

Following the forcible crushing of the Hungarian Revolution in 1956, Soviet ideologists had developed the term "socialist commonwealth" in a somewhat conciliatory sense, in part to justify the Soviet Union's intervention, but perhaps more to rebuild or to cultivate for the first time meaningful ties of community and consensus. Twelve years later, however, that doctrine took on an ominous quality. Now it constituted a threat to independent behavior and was contrasted to the notion—used pejoratively—of "national sovereignty." The interests of the whole, Moscow warned, had to override particularism. And these interests, it was clear, were to be decided and formulated first and foremost by the prevailing preferences in Moscow.

The new order imposed in Eastern Europe by the Kremlin may have been superficially effective, but it left unsettled a series of difficult problems whose implications extended to the Soviet Union itself. First, the Soviets—while crushing and at least containing the Czechoslovak road to socialism—did not put an end to nationalist sentiments in Eastern Europe and at home. Rather, it might be presumed that one result of the invasion was increased resentment against Great Russian chauvinism throughout the area and in the border regions of the Soviet Union. Second, experimentation in economic affairs was still permitted, and many

East Europeans (as well as western observers) believed that alterations in the material base might yet lead to major shake-ups in the political superstructure. Third, though many East European intellectuals felt intimidated by the rapid, surgical, and comprehensive measures carried out against Czechoslovakia, their alienation from Moscow's satrapies probably deepened. This resentment, suppressed for the present, might explode in the future whether Soviet-sponsored controls are tightened or loosened. Finally—a mixed blessing for the Soviets—their actions against Czechoslovakia imparted a breath of life into the western alliance at a moment when its future looked dim. As might have been expected, the communist parties in the West lost some supporters and suffered significant attrition in their ranks as a result of the Soviet invasion in Czechoslovakia.

## THE CHANGING ROLE OF "HOSTAGE EUROPE" IN SOVIET STRATEGIC POLICIES

The prospect of greater West European unity in the late 1960s did not disturb Moscow in the way that it had in the mid-1950s. Using Western Europe as a hostage to prevent an American strike against the Soviet Union was no longer so important to Moscow's security. The main reason for this is that, by the late 1960s, the Soviet Union had acquired an assured destruction capability against the United States to supplement that which had been acquired many years earlier with regard to Western Europe. Furthermore, the fact that West Germany signed the Nonproliferation Treaty helped reduce the potential threat that the Soviet Union might feel from West Europe as opposed to the United

States. Indeed, the main threat from West Germany appeared to be more of a political-economic nature than of an active military-strategic one. In fact, the more immediate challenges to Soviet security interests came from within the erstwhile Soviet empire and from the international communist movement: in Eastern Europe, in the form of political and ideological challenges; and in the Far East, from a revisionist China complaining about inequities in the Sino-Soviet frontier regions and emboldened by a steadily expanding nuclear and missile capability.

Granted this apparent decline of Western Europe's importance as a hostage, it nonetheless could still become overnight the focal point of renewed cold war tensions. This possibility, however remote, stems mainly from the indeterminate political situation in Germany, which still prevails more than two decades after the end of World War II.

West European unity or disunity in the economic and technological realms may also affect the situation. If a movement toward unity and cooperation should again become evident, this would likely stimulate the interests of East European countries in participating in the Common Market, which would likely produce Soviet and, perhaps, East German consternation. If West European unity or living standards should decline, however, the magnetic attraction of Western Europe to the East would also weaken. During the early 1970s, however, the most likely trend may be a continuation of the present situation, in which Western Europe's living standards generally grow at a faster rate than Eastern Europe's, but without any important strengthening of the institutions of European unity. Depending on the extent of this gap between eastern and western living standards, the East Europeans may feel either despair or, alternatively, a sensation of confidence linked with rising demands.

## CHANGING SOVIET VIEWS ON REQUISITES
## OF EUROPEAN SECURITY

Though Europe's relative significance has decreased in Soviet eyes, its absolute importance remains. Because of various historical reasons, as well as its geographical proximity, Europe is viewed by the Soviet Union as crucial to its security. Hence, any consideration of Moscow's over-all views on strategy and arms control must take into account Soviet views on Europe, as well as the superpower strategic balance, Sino-Soviet relations, and other problems.

For several decades, at least, Soviet views on the requisites of European security have involved a fundamental ambiguity: whether to seek Russian hegemony over all of Europe, or to work toward some form of condominium at the superpower level. A further ambiguity is embodied in the Warsaw Treaty itself. The very document that sets up the framework of the Soviet-led military alliance system also looks forward to the demise of the system and its replacement by an all-European system of collective defense.[1] Since the establishment of the Warsaw Pact in 1955, the Soviet Union and its allies have frequently proposed putting an end to the two military blocs confronting each other

[1] For a text of the Warsaw Treaty, see *New Times* (Moscow), no. 21 (May 21, 1955), pp. 65–69. See specifically Articles IX and XI.

in Europe. Such proposals emanated, for example, from the meeting of Warsaw Pact members in Bucharest on July 5, 1966, and were contained in the resolutions of the Conference of European Communist and Workers Parties in Karlovy Vary, which met April 24 to 26, 1967.[2]

These ideas were also repeated recently in various Soviet statements, including an article in *Pravda* on January 8, 1969, by Yuri Zhukov, entitled "Europe: Ripening Problems." Such proposals, Zhukov noted, were not new, but their urgency had become greater because of current problems and tensions. Zhukov's article was ostensibly stimulated in part by an announcement, early in 1969, that an all-European conference had been called for October 1969, by public figures from nineteen European countries and representatives of several international organizations who had met in Vienna. The two major aims of this conference, Zhukov noted, would be to create a system of collective security and to promote close collaboration among European states in the interests of peace and disarmament.

## THE PROBLEM OF GERMANY IN LONG-RANGE SOVIET POLICY

The salience of Germany in Soviet discussions of European security is not surprising, for Germany has been a central factor influencing Russian policy since well before the October 1917 revolution. Indeed, the most

[2] For details, see Marshall D. Shulman, "A European Security Conference," *Survival*, vol. XI, no. 12 (December 1969), p. 373–81.

important variable in European international politics for over fifty years has been the state of Soviet-German relations. The nature of these relations has been an overriding consideration in determining whether there would be war or peace, alliance or conflict, arms control or an arms race in Europe. Disagreements among the occupying powers over the management of the German problem, for instance, were an important early factor stimulating the emergence of the Cold War in the late 1940s. Subsequently, the fear that an armed West Germany might enter the European Defense Community and NATO spurred the Kremlin to major policy shifts. Beginning in 1952 and continuing through the Geneva summit and Adenauer's visit to Moscow in September 1955, the Soviets dangled before the western alliance the prospect of a reunited, but neutral, Germany. To buttress their bargaining position, the Soviets threatened to establish their own multilateral alliance system, which they did in May 1955, and—when it appeared that Bonn would proceed with appropriate funding for the *Bundeswehr*—they conferred on the German Democratic Republic equal status with other members of the Warsaw Pact in 1956. Since that time, the Soviets have frequently evinced their determination to obtain full recognition for East Germany, their alleged desire to regularize the questions still unsettled since the end of World War II, and their serious concern about the introduction of tactical nuclear weapons into the European theatre and the possibility that West Germany might obtain direct access to nuclear weapons.

The nature of Moscow's policies, to be sure, is open to divergent interpretations. It appears, nonetheless, that Moscow has frequently been willing to pay a rather high price to neutralize a potential military threat from West Germany. Soviet statements and behavior patterns between 1952 and 1955 suggested a willingness to sacrifice East German interests if West Germany could be kept from membership in NATO and prevented from possessing or having access to nuclear weapons. This line of thinking was discouraged by the West's cool response to such suggestions, and also by Moscow's rising confidence, after 1957–58, about its bargaining position—an attitude more conducive to threats than to offers of compromise.

The contradictory nature of Soviet policy toward West Germany can be partially illustrated by using some concepts of game theory. The stakes in such a contest are extremely high; the response of the adversary is uncertain; and the pursuit of one strategy tends to negate prospects of achieving success with the other. Can this be kept to a two-person game or must many players participate? If the latter, the number of variables and possible outcomes increases geometrically. Logical decision-making is difficult because of the high emotional content introduced into any consideration of German-Soviet relations. Bitter memories from the past intrude to affect calculations about the present and the future. As a result, Soviet policy has continued to vacillate between frontal pressures and seductive hints about the possible merits of a Moscow-Bonn axis.[3]

[3] A commemorative volume marking the fortieth anniversary of the Rapallo Treaty was published by Soviet and East German scholars in 1962. See A. Anderle and G. N. Goroshkova (eds.), *Rapallskii dogovor i problema mirnogo sosushchestovovaniia*

The analysis by an outsider of Soviet views toward West Germany is the more complicated because of the difficulty in distinguishing between real and ostensible Soviet fears of German revanchism. The history of centuries demonstrates that Russia does have cause to fear military aggression or, at a minimum, economic penetration from Germany. West Germany enjoys a powerful economic, political, and even military potential that could conceivably be brought to bear against the countries of the Warsaw Pact. For the present, the military aspect of this potential seems to be under control—whether by the West European Union, the United States, the terms of a Nonproliferation Treaty, or even, if necessary, preventive intervention of Soviet power. There are presently only two nations which enjoy superpower status, and neither of these seems willing or likely to permit a resurgence of German militarism. Although interpretations of this subject vary considerably, it also appears that the West German leaders and population as a whole would oppose any attempt to engage in military competition with the East.

There seems little doubt that Soviet and some East European leaders deliberately exaggerate the threat of West German revanchism to justify certain totalitarian practices and the hardships imposed on the countries of the Warsaw Pact. They do this also in order to cause alienation among the NATO countries. Nevertheless, it appears safe to assume that there is a fundamental and deep-seated anxiety—not only in Moscow but in other East European capitals—about West Germany. It is a

(The Rapallo Treaty and the Problem of Peaceful Coexistence) (Moscow, 1963). See also I. K. Kobliakov, *Ot Bresta do Rapallo* (From Brest to Rapallo) (Moscow, 1954).

kind of X-factor which must be respected. One can imagine scenarios in which West Germany would play a catalytic role bringing the West into a major war with the eastern countries. But there may be other courses of action equally dangerous for the security of the eastern nations which cannot be clearly discerned. Prudence dictates that measures be taken to obviate the necessity of unilateral action by any country against West Germany. Preventive diplomacy should be much easier to exercise than preventive war. Should the Soviet Union become increasingly engaged in its difficulties with China or should the United States withdraw from Europe, the possibility of independent action by Germany might increase—hence Moscow's determination to prevent the development of any sequence of events which could cause that long-range threat to become a reality.

While the long-range danger of West Germany's military potential is real enough to the Soviet Union, a much more immediate problem for Moscow is the economic and political influence exerted by Bonn in Eastern Europe.[4] The flexible *Ostpolitik* adopted since 1966 has deprived Moscow and other East European capitals of grist for propaganda about the aggressive intentions of the Federal Republic. Indeed, it seems unfortunate that Bonn's recalcitrance on some issues— especially the Oder-Neisse line and the Munich Treaty —provided Warsaw Pact ideologues with any concrete issues for their arguments about the revisionist quality

[4] For documentation on Weimar Germany's plans to use economic levers to wrest political concessions from Poland and Czechoslovakia, see *Journal of Central European Affairs*, vol. XXI, no. 1 (April 1961), pp. 15–44.

of the Kiesinger-Brandt *Ostpolitik*.[5] Both these themes
—fear of German flexibility coupled with an attempt
to exploit the harder-line aspects of West German diplomacy—recurred frequently, for example, in the discussion of European security and relations between
states of the two systems at an April 1968 conference
in Moscow.[6]

Many of the events preceding the invasion of Czechoslovakia demonstrated the lengths to which conservatives in the Warsaw Pact nations would go to use the
alleged military threat of West Germany as a pretext
for obstructing what was probably their much more
real concern, namely, the momentum of economic and
even diplomatic relationships building between the
Pact countries and the Federal Republic. Probably the
outstanding examples of these propaganda devices were
the alleged finds of arms caches ostensibly planted by
West German agents and reported first of all in the
Soviet and the Bulgarian press.

The ability of East Germany to affect the over-all

[5] Theo Sommer has argued that Bonn should make clear that
it seeks not a territorial but a qualitative change in the status
quo; that it is prepared to respect Russian security interests,
though it would wish to see no Soviet interference in the process
toward ideological diversity within Moscow's sphere of power,
and, consequently, in the contacts between East and West. See *Die
Zeit,* September 20, 1968.

[6] The proceedings are summarized in the journal *Mirovaia
ekonomika i mezhdunarodnye otnosheniia* (World Economy and
International Relations), no. 7 (1968), pp. 102–20, and in no.
8 (1968), pp. 72–81. The head of the Polish delegation at this
conference, for example, addressed himself to the new eastern
policy of the Federal Republic—"myths and actuality." (*Ibid.,*
no. 7, pp. 117–18.)

state of East-West relations should not be underestimated. Pankow's anxieties but also its political muscle were demonstrated after the establishment of East German-Rumanian relations in January 1967. Between March and September of that same year the East German government had secured treaties of friendship and mutual assistance with Poland, Czechoslovakia, Hungary, and Bulgaria. (A similar treaty had been signed with Moscow in June 1964.) East Germany's diplomatic leverage was still more conspicuous when its officials added to traffic controls between West Germany and Berlin in early summer 1968, an action that probably came more at Pankow's initiative than at Moscow's. Later that summer, the East German leaders were probably even more influential than the Polish in pressing Moscow for armed intervention in Czechoslovakia.

By late 1969 it appeared that Moscow was again prepared to override the preferences of the East German government. Nevertheless, the danger remained that, if tension develops between East and West, Pankow may seek to exacerbate in ways that would strengthen and demonstrate its authority. If there is détente, the East German government, fearing for its *raison d'être*, may endeavor to obstruct rapprochement. Somewhat in the way that Moscow once feared Bonn could ignite a catalytic war, all parties must be concerned lest Pankow heighten tensions to promote its special interests. At the same time, the West must look for possible solutions to the German problem that could prove acceptable to the East German regime and helpful to the political and economic conditions of the people of East Germany.

163

The immediate, nonmilitary challenge of West Germany to Soviet interests in Eastern Europe probably presents the Kremlin with a much less tractable problem than the hypothetical long-range prospect of a revival of German militarism. This immediate problem, naturally, profoundly affects the immediate outlook for maintaining or expanding Soviet influence in Europe.

## PRESENT PRIORITIES AND FUTURE OPTIONS

In trying to project future Soviet behavior, we must begin by evaluating the goals of the Soviet leadership, the challenges and opportunities likely to be available to effect these goals, and finally—depending on the particular conditions that actually emerge—the alternate future strategies that Moscow may pursue. The historical record suggests that, at least since the death of Stalin in 1953, Soviet leaders have agreed on three values that their policies should promote. These have existed in a certain rank order: first, maintenance of the security of the Soviet state and the CPSU regime; second, maintenance and, if possible, strengthening of Soviet hegemony in Eastern Europe; third, and less tangible, maintenance and strengthening of the living standards of the Soviet people.

In pursuit of these objectives, a number of subordinate goals have also been sought. These lesser goals are, in a sense, ends in themselves, but, in another sense, they are also means or instruments by which to achieve the more important and enduring priorities: first, strengthening the Soviet armed forces to deter external attack and to intervene abroad if necessary to promote Soviet interests; second, strengthening the Soviet economy—particularly heavy industry—so as to serve the military requirements of the state and to contribute to a stronger base for the development of consumer goods; third, maintenance of stable relations with the United States and the achievement of arms controls conducive to international security; fourth, the cultivation of communist and revolutionary activities abroad within the limitations established by the desire for international security, but also with some restraints so as to minimize damage to other objectives.

The importance of both Western and Eastern Europe in this hierarchy of ends and means is quite fundamental, even though, as noted earlier, other geographical areas and functional problems have risen in salience relative to Europe. If we look at Soviet policy toward Europe, however, we begin to understand the tension between some of these priorities and some of the Soviet instruments for achieving them. As we consider the problem more deeply, it appears that many priorities turn out to be mutually antithetical so that progress toward one makes it more difficult or even impossible to achieve success in another. Thus, it is of primary importance to Moscow that there be no military threat to its interests emanating from Europe. Yet, if Moscow seeks to achieve this objective by a relaxation of tensions with the West European countries and by the establishment of certain forms of arms control, the conditions and atmosphere that follow may well make it more difficult to promote the second objective—maintenance and strengthening of Soviet influence in Eastern Europe. Also, it is fairly easy to envisage scenarios in which progress toward the first or second priority might undermine the Kremlin's ability to enhance its influence in the international communist movement.

The major options open to the Soviet leadership in

the present and in the near-to-intermediate future may be categorized in terms of four models. Each model represents a future course that the Kremlin may wish to pursue, given changes in the nature and mix of the various components determining Soviet policy. These alternate futures are discussed here in terms of their relative likelihood, considering the opportunities for and constraints upon Soviet policy-makers in the early 1970s:

1. Preserving the status quo;
2. A strategy of interdependence;
3. Indirect advance;
4. A forward strategy; and
5. Isolationism.

In discussing the options open to the Soviet leaders, we do so with the recognition that these are abstractions, and that in fact elements of each course may be present in Soviet behavior. On the other hand, this procedure seems recommended by the history of Soviet foreign policy, which is indeed replete with periods in which one or the other strategy has gained the upper hand. As Marshall Shulman has suggested:

> What the analyst seeks to do, but not to overdo, is to identify the dominant tendency at any one time and the shifts in policy emphasis which make for the recurrent pattern in Soviet behavior. . . . The analyst, if he happens to be interested in the quantification of human behavior, should not expect to find emerging on his drum chart the regular curves of a pulsing alternation. Since the determination of these choices involves a process of interaction with the events and circumstances of the outside world as these appear to the decision makers

166

in Moscow, one cannot predict the duration or the amplitude or the direction of future cycles. However, this kind of analysis does provide a framework which helps us to interpret isolated data and to distinguish cyclical from evolutionary changes.[7]

Shulman's words were directed to the analysis of history, but they seem to apply with even greater force to attempts at setting out the alternative courses which Moscow may pursue given certain developments in years to come.

Aspects of each model have been present in past Soviet policies. It is feasible (though not easy) for many of these elements to coexist simultaneously and symbiotically. It is quite possible, however, that Moscow may emphasize a particular course in dealing with one aspect of its European policy, but another course in dealing with a different geographical area or a certain functional problem in Europe. In 1955, for example, the Soviet Union withdrew from Austria; buttressed Soviet influence in Eastern Europe by creating the Warsaw Pact; tendered to Titoist Yugoslavia a new aura of ideological acceptability; and took steps to spawn in western imaginations a notion of a bomber gap—all the while laying the ground for a rapid buildup of Soviet influence in the Third World, particularly in the Middle East. Nevertheless, for analytical purposes, it seems worthwhile to discuss each of the five alternatives separately so that we can understand the circumstances most likely to evoke particular strains of Soviet action. We begin with what appears to be Moscow's most probable course—preserving the status quo.

[7] *Stalin's Foreign Policy Reappraised* (Cambridge, Mass.: Harvard University Press, 1963), pp. 6–7.

## The Status Quo

Since the Treaty of Brest-Litovsk, a recurring theme in Soviet European policy has been an effort to maintain the status quo, territorially and politically. Frequently behind this strategy has been the notion that the Soviet Union should buy time in order to build up its power base for a forward strategy at some later time. On many occasions prior to World War II, a status quo strategy was pursued primarily because the Soviet Union was weak. Thus, in the 1920s Soviet ideologues spoke of the "temporary stabilization of capitalism" and the phenomenon of "socialism in one country." From 1934 to 1938, Soviet spokesmen endorsed collective security against territorial revisionism. Even the Ribbentrop-Molotov accord of 1939 was motivated in large part by a concern to preserve the status quo, though the Kremlin certainly welcomed the territorial gains which accrued as a by-product of this understanding. The common element in these Soviet policies of the 1920s and 1930s was Moscow's desire to obtain a "breathing space" uninterrupted by foreign intervention.

Many facets of Moscow's post-World War II policies are also consonant with the notion of a status quo model. Even the sovietization and communization of the East European countries may be viewed as a way of consolidating what had become a new status quo after the war, a way of ensuring that the area did not revert to being a launching pad for military threats against the Soviet Union. The interventions in Hungary and in Czechoslovakia in 1956 and in 1968 were holding operations rather than actions designed to alter the international balance of power. Even Soviet pressures against West Berlin and Moscow's various ultimatums aimed at a peace treaty to settle the questions remaining from World War II appear to have been motivated more by a concern to consolidate and protect the fruits of that war than by the desire to inaugurate a new round of conflict aimed at subjugating additional areas of Europe to Soviet domination.

Soviet policy toward Eastern Europe since World War II continues to be motivated by a kind of weakness—a fear that Russia's influence in the area rests on fragile foundations that can be undermined either by unrest within the region or by provocative interventions from without. On the other hand, the post-1945 territorial-political arrangement in Eastern Europe has rounded out the frontiers once controlled by tsarist Russia and gone on to include Rumania and Bulgaria in the south and an important part of Germany in the north. This situation differs in important respects from that of the more isolated and more vulnerable Soviet Union of the interwar years. The Soviet Union of the 1920s and the 1930s had lost and failed to win back much of the domain ruled by the tsars, and it probably looked forward to the day when those territories could be reincorporated under Moscow's rule. In this sense, the territorial extension of the Soviet Union today is undoubtedly much more acceptable to the Soviet hierarchy than was that of the interwar period. Nevertheless, the Soviet position in Eastern Europe continues to rest upon rather fragile bases. Both economically and ideologically the Soviet Union and the governments allied with it are in a rather weak position vis-à-vis the West. Indeed, the ideological premises that the Prague reformers turned to in

169

1968 resembled reincarnations of nineteenth-century liberalism and the social democratic variant of Marxism which became anathema to Lenin and his followers. Added to relative economic weakness, ideological decay, and political disarray are the various constraints upon Soviet policy noted in the foregoing section—particularly, the deep suspicion with which West Europeans view Soviet overtures and their greater willingness to cooperate with the United States. In these circumstances, Moscow's strategy may seek to rebuild the foundations of Soviet influence in Eastern Europe while sealing off the area from western penetration.

## Interdependence

The next most likely Soviet strategy appears to be one based on a concept of interdependence or, at least, collaboration with the western powers. The objective of this strategy would not be to oust the United States from Europe, but rather to obtain a viable working relationship with the United States to cope with the political and security problems of the area. This approach would be in a sense a revival of the wartime entente or of the policy direction that showed signs of fruition in 1955 and in 1963. Acceptance of this model in the foreseeable future, even if it could succeed, would be extremely difficult, however, mainly because of the risk that it would stimulate centrifugal forces of disintegration in Eastern Europe. This model would presumably open the door to bridge-building tactics by the West, precisely of the kind that have been condemned in numerous Soviet statements.[8]

On the other hand, Moscow might decide to take

[8] See, for example, *Komsomolskaia Pravda*, October 6, 1968;

this risk if it felt that it had indeed consolidated communist power once again in Eastern Europe and that the time had come to deal constructively and creatively with the German problem. Assuming that it gave up any hope of dealing with Germany in a repressive manner, Moscow might well decide that a negotiated package would satisfy the vital interests of the parties concerned and provide a more solid foundation for peace in Europe. Such an orientation could be spurred (1) by heightened Soviet fears of China or of an American or Japanese rapprochement with China, (2) by a desire to unite with the other northern industrialized nations to maintain order and perhaps to help promote development of the Third World, and (3) by a *sine qua non*—a willingness in the West to make constructive initiatives and to respond to Soviet proposals in a manner calculated to cope with the vital interests of all parties and to avoid exploiting Soviet vulnerabilities in Eastern Europe. For such an orientation to arise on both sides probably would presume some stabilization of the strategic arms race so that the superpowers and, presumably, their allies would feel safe. The most profound obstacle to a strategy of interdependence is, as suggested before, that progress toward a real sense of international security in Europe might weaken Soviet influence and communist institutions generally in Eastern Europe.

## Indirect Advance

Somewhat less likely, instead of focusing on maintenance of the status quo or on improving relations

---

*Pravda*, November 22, 1968; *Sovetskaia Rossia*, November 22, 1968; *Pravda*, November 13, 1968.

with the West, the Soviet Union might endeavor to expand its sphere of influence westward. Her minimum objective would be to weaken or even remove U.S. military forces from the Continent, turning Europe toward a more neutral zone between the superpowers. Once this happened, a more far-reaching goal might become feasible: Soviet domination of all Europe.

Such a strategy could be motivated by ideology, by realpolitik, or—most likely—by some admixture of these and other factors.[9] The tactics employed could be "rightist" or "leftist," corresponding to the terms "indirect advance" or "forward strategy" used in this chapter. As Marshall Shulman has pointed out, Soviet policy has often alternated between recurrent patterns involving "two marked syndromes of behavior—one that is essentially militant and direct, the other manipulative, flexible, and longer-term in perspective."[10] Either approach could be utilized for defensive as well as for offensive purposes. Thus Soviet agitation for disarmament in the 1920s, one study has argued, constituted "a tactic in a grand strategy which, while defensive in the short run, was meant to be offensive in the long run . . . the continuation of revolution by other means."[11]

A soviet political offensive against Europe in the early 1970s would probably rely on rightist rather than

[9] For a discussion of underlying factors in Soviet decision-making, see Walter C. Clemens, Jr., *The Arms Race and Sino-Soviet Relations* (Stanford, Cal: The Hoover Institution on War, Revolution, and Peace, 1968), pp. 231ff.

[10] *Stalin's Foreign Policy Reappraised*, pp. 4–9.

[11] Walter C. Clemens, Jr., "Lenin and Disarmament," *Slavic Review*, vol. XXIII, no. 3 (September 1964), p. 525.

on leftist tactics. It would endeavor to lull the suspicions of West Europeans about Soviet intentions and to sharpen their dislike for U.S. influences. Peace propaganda, gestures respecting the grandeur of national culture, promises of economic benefit and technological collaboration—these would be the most likely themes in Moscow's approach.

If the rightist syndrome were used, it would resemble in important respects a status quo or interdependence strategy. A policy of preserving the status quo, however, would be more inward looking, more cautious, and more defensive. It would shy away from the more open and risky tactics needed to penetrate the reserve of Western Europe. A strategy of interdependence would differ from an indirect advance in that it would look to cooperative rather than hegemonic relations with the West; the most visible manifestation of this difference would be a less hostile attitude toward the United States. A Soviet proposal for an all-European security system, for example, might in principle be consonant with either strategy. If Moscow were aiming at domination of Europe, however, the tone and content of the negotiations would necessarily be quite different from those which anticipated a partnership with Europe and, *a fortiori,* with the United States. A shrewdly designed rightist syndrome might begin with a tone that stressed cooperation, shifting later to a content designed to facilitate Soviet hegemony.

For Moscow to decide on an indirect advance, it would have to become rather confident about its ability to withstand the reverberations that might result both in the Soviet Union and Eastern Europe. To begin with, the Soviet leaders would have to detect signs that the United States might be willing to withdraw from Europe or that enough anti-American sentiment could be mobilized to compel it to do so. No less problematical, Moscow would presumably need some assurance that, minus the United States, it could dominate Germany and other West European powers—rather than the other way around.

## A Forward Strategy

Still more remote is the prospect that the Kremlin would revert to a forward strategy based on the kind of leftist tactics that came to the fore in 1917 to 1921, 1928 to 1933, and 1946 to 1948, or, to a much lesser extent, in 1958 to 1961. Moscow seems less likely to rely upon subversion, threats, or revolutionary appeals —in part because Western Europe has become more stable and more difficult to influence in any radical way, and in part because history shows that Soviet pressures generate reactions and counterpressures that become detrimental to Soviet interests.

It is difficult to plot the kind of circumstances that would encourage the Kremlin to attempt a leftist advance. The most encouraging event might be the accomplished fact of a U.S. military withdrawal to Fortress America, a prospect that does not appear likely in the near to intermediate future. Apart from this, extreme political and economic weaknesses in Europe, particularly if accompanied by a U.S. withdrawal, might create a revolutionary situation that Moscow could seek to exploit. In addition, should Germany move sharply toward a militarist posture, Moscow might attempt a kind of preventive action summoning popular forces in various European countries to the same cause. A leftist strategy might also be encouraged by rising opposition to Soviet rule at home and in East European states. Any of these scenarios would presume considerable quiet on the Sino-Soviet frontier—even a reconciliation with Peking—and Soviet indifference about the sentiments of bourgeois nationalist regimes in the Third World.

Alarm over ideological erosion at home might bring to power a more militant and doctrinaire faction, intent on reviving the revolutionary movement in Europe, partly so as to justify a more vigilant posture domestically. This kind of grouping could count on the support of some military leaders if it could be demonstrated that West Germany were again threatening the Soviet Union. Otherwise, even if the voice of military interests should increase in party circles, this would by no means ensure a more forward strategy, but would more likely consolidate the forces in favor of securing the status quo.

## Isolationism

The least likely Soviet strategy is a dominant trend toward withdrawal. To be sure, the status quo policy presumes a kind of withdrawal from intervention in Western Europe, but it also implies more intensive Soviet involvement in Eastern Europe. The basic reason why isolationism seems improbable is that great powers, once committed, tend to remain so—particularly in a geographically contiguous and strategically important area. Moscow's determination to remain in

Eastern Europe was evidenced, of course, by the intervention in Czechoslovakia, and by the justification—in ideological and quasi-legal terms known as the Brezhnev Doctrine. But Moscow also made clear its minimum goal of denying a key strategic area to the West and retaining it under Soviet influence.

Nevertheless, a number of contingencies can be envisaged, which, if they become more salient, might at least contribute to a heightened Soviet disinclination toward involvement in the affairs of Western and even of Eastern Europe:

1. Rising consumer demands and political dissidence within the Soviet Union;
2. Rising costs of supporting and influencing the East European regimes;
3. A growing gap in living standards and ideologies between East and West;
4. Increasing friction and potential dangers in Sino-Soviet relations;
5. Diminished military threat potential of Western Europe;
6. Deployment of an ABM system capable of defending the Soviet Union against low-grade attacks from European or Chinese forces;
7. Mutual, stabilized deterrence in Soviet-American strategic relations;
8. Lessened Soviet interest in the Third World (or, alternatively, a belief that penetration of some areas such as the Middle East or the Indian subcontinent might bring greater rewards than comparable efforts in Eastern or Western Europe) ; and

9. Erosion of communist ideology at home and in Europe.

Most of these contingencies are not antithetical. If many of them occurred simultaneously, they would reinforce one another, leading to a reduced Soviet willingness to take risks and to make expenditures necessary to strengthen or even maintain Soviet influence in Europe.

One variant of this strategy should also be noted, however, which could follow logically and chronologically from the success of another strategy: that of interdependence. If cooperation with the West led to a settlement of the problems associated with a divided Germany and with a Europe divided into opposing military blocs, Moscow might feel that it could afford to withdraw at least some of its military forces now deployed in Eastern Europe. Indeed, the settlement might even specify such a withdrawal, though some forces might have to remain as part of a guarantee system.

### Conclusions and Implications for Arms Control

The preceding analysis examined five alternative Soviet strategies toward Europe. Each of these strategies reflects certain Soviet objectives and actions as shaped by domestic, intrabloc, European, and global policy considerations, opportunities, and constraints. Because the various security and political arrangements in Europe since 1945 have not led to open warfare there and may have helped to prevent such a conflict, there is a reluctance on all sides to abolish, or deviate from, a system that has "worked." This reluctance helps to explain why the Soviet Union, among other powers, is highly committed to a policy of preserving the status quo.

On the other hand, we have had since 1945, not one, but a series of changing European security systems, expressed not only in the evolution of bilateral and multilateral alliances, but also in the dynamics of the military balance and in the nuances of the international political climate. These instabilities have in turn been reflected in pendulum shifts in the strategic doctrines of the superpowers and their allies. What has remained constant, however, is the polarization of the European nations into two camps, each led by a superpower, the influence of which has varied with time and place.

A continued Soviet policy of status quo in Europe will be shaped, as before, by important Soviet policy objectives, external constraints, and perceptions of the risks, costs, and gains inherent in such a policy. Thus, Soviet policy toward Europe is largely shaped by defensive security considerations; by the desire to retain hegemony in Eastern Europe; by the need to contain political, economic, and psychological pressures on Eastern Europe from the West, mainly from West Germany; and by the desire to retain policy options and flexibility vis-à-vis Western Europe, while seeking strategic arms control agreements with the United States. Some of the problems for Soviet policy-makers created by this set of goals derive from the fact that some aspects of Moscow's strategy tend to undermine the utility of other policy objectives. Thus, the prospect of a useful superpower arms control agreement may intensify Soviet control problems in Eastern Europe and may also increase West German pressures for increased, independent military capabilities. Moreover, the alternative possibility of some Soviet-West German accommodation could create strong resentment among some East Europeans toward Moscow. The problem for the Soviet Union, therefore, is how to contain East European pressures for greater independence and West German political and military aspirations and flexible *Ostpolitik,* while at the same time seeking strategic arms control agreements with the United States.

The Soviet Union has in recent years gained a broader margin of leverage in its policy toward Europe. The creation of a more credible strategic deterrence capability vis-à-vis the United States has enabled the Soviets, in principle, to pursue a more flexible policy in Europe in the search for political gains while its basic strategic security needs are ensured through the stable deterrence relationship with the United States.

What then are the implications for arms control of a Soviet policy of status quo in Europe? First, the preservation of Soviet interests in Eastern Europe, the denial of nuclear access to West Germany, and the initiation of Soviet-American strategic arms control talks seem to be high priority objectives of Soviet policy. It is highly unlikely that the current Soviet regime would undertake any action which would threaten the first two of these objectives, and, therefore, any success in the impending arms control talks will have to accommodate these Soviet interests.

Second, though a long-range settlement of outstanding European security problems could best be achieved through a Soviet strategy of interdependence, the chances for such a strategy in the short run are probably less likely than for that of status quo. Despite

179

fervent Warsaw Pact appeals for an all-European security system, disagreements and uncertainties within the Soviet alliance system on this subject may equal those in the West. What is desirable, in short, may not be feasible without a good deal more long-range planning on all sides.

Soviet relations with Eastern Europe and West Germany will play an important role in future Soviet-American strategic arms control talks, and these relations, in turn, will be strongly affected by the outcome of the talks. A successfully negotiated freeze of strategic forces, for example, would enhance Soviet conventional capabilities and would offer greater maneuverability in dealing with the East European states (and with Communist China) . An arms freeze could, at the same time, increase the level of political activism of the East Europeans vis-à-vis Moscow. The failure to achieve any significant strategic arms control agreement could lead to a new intensification of European relations, within and between the blocs, and might generate dangerous levels of political and military instability in that region. Recognizing the many obstacles to such an accord, all parties may still find that the best way to deal with European security and arms control problems is through an all-European arrangement with some form of superpower participation.

# 6

## Conclusions and Projections

SOVIET ARMS CONTROL MOTIVES are complex and ambiguous. Moreover, arms control issues involve a variety of technological, military, political, economic, and psychological factors which are frequently at odds with one another. Indeed, the impetus for arms control is rather fragile and ephemeral: if the circumstances for such negotiations are propitious at one time, they may be rapidly overtaken by events, by the inexorable march of technology and shifts in the psychological milieu.

Certain recent developments, however, contribute to a climate conducive to arms control. Key among them is the realization, in the words of President Nixon, that "the traditional course of seeking security primarily through military strength raises several problems in a world of multiplying strategic weapons." President Nixon went on to enumerate the problems: "Modern technology makes any balance precarious and prompts new efforts at ever higher levels of complexity. Such an arms race absorbs resources, talents, and energies."

181

Increased complexity leads to greater "uncertainty about the other side's intentions," and "the higher [the] level of armaments, the greater the violence and devastation, should deterrence fail."[1] Similarly sober views on the futility and dangers of building ever greater and newer strategic inventories are constantly echoed by the Soviet leaders and by the Soviet press. Yet, as McGeorge Bundy asserted, "there is a curious and distressing paradox in all this. The same political leaders who know these terrible weapons must never be used and who do not run the foolish risks of nuclear gamesmanship abroad still do not hesitate to authorize system after system."[2]

While Bundy's observation about the gap between political rhetoric and policy behavior is well founded, it seems too harsh. The fact is that proposals for Soviet-American arms control measures are cast in a world conditioned by intense East-West hostility, by past and current major conflicts of vital interests, by psychological resistance to trusting the adversary, and, most of all, by deep uncertainties about the implementation and outcome of the unprecedented arrangements that may emerge from the talks. Moreover, such proposals evoke profound uneasiness among the major institutions whose past *raison d'être* has been to create fear in the adversary, lest he consider aggressive measures.

The wall of distrust must be scaled, however, if for no other reason than because the world of the 1970s

[1] A report to the Congress by Richard Nixon, President of the United States, *U.S. Foreign Policy for the 1970s; A New Strategy for Peace,* February 18, 1970, p. 142.

[2] McGeorge Bundy, "To Cap the Volcano," *Foreign Affairs,* no. 1 (October 1969).

will be different in many ways from that of past decades. The basic difference is that the United States and the Soviet Union have become strategic equals, and whatever the technological and numerical advances achieved in either country, their relationship will not change significantly in the foreseeable future.

## FACTORS MOTIVATING SOVIET ARMS CONTROL INTERESTS

The likely motivations for serious Soviet interest in arms control can be broken down into three groups: objective motives (derived from perceptions of likely gains in military, political, and economic areas) ; subjective motives (generated by uncertainties and concerns about a new unchecked arms-race cycle) ; and manipulative motives (aimed at creating "favorable" political and psychological conditions in the West relevant to arms control) .

Many Soviet leaders see a new arms race with the United States as both militarily and politically unproductive—and possibly counterproductive—while at the same time creating new and undesirable demands on their internal resources. They seem to believe that since both superpowers now possess assured destruction capabilities (though asymmetrical ones) , it makes little sense to continue to increase significantly their strategic offensive and defensive forces in an open-ended manner. Therefore, since both superpowers are vitally concerned about retaining a stable and credible deterrence relation, it is useless and possibly dangerous to consider the actual deployment of potentially destabilizing weapons systems. Such an eventuality could possibly provoke the reemergence of the surprise-attack fears that pervaded the security perceptions of both super-powers during the 1950s when the "balance of terror" was considered indeed "delicate."

A stabilization of the arms race at mutually accepta-ble levels would tend to enhance other Soviet policy interests, which have increased in recent years, and actually increase the options for dealing with them. The Soviet Union has extended its political and military influence in the Mediterranean and the Middle East, and its interest in the Persian Gulf and North African areas is mounting. Moreover, the deteriorating situation on the Sino-Soviet border and related complications have introduced new demands and stresses on Soviet military capabilities. Thus, Soviet defense capabilities are being spread out, both for offensive and defensive reasons, in the face of new demands on resources in connection with the Soviet-American armed balance. A stabilization of the strategic arms competition would logically ease the pressures on Soviet resources and commitments, since current and foreseeable Soviet policy interests necessitate largely the support of con-ventional, rather than strategic nuclear, forces.

Turning to the subjective Soviet motives, it appears that Soviet leaders are becoming concerned with certain developments in the United States which harbor poten-tial challenges to them. Policy decisions concerning the expansion of the Safeguard ABM system and the poten-tial deployment of the Poseidon and Minuteman III MIRV systems suggest to the Soviets a renewed hard-ening of the U.S. position—a return to a policy "from a position of force" and a search for strategic superiority and renewed threat of first-strike planning. This in-terpretation is supported by various public statements by leading U.S. governmental figures. The Soviets give the impression that they are unaware that their own expanding SS-9 missile system, in addition to increases in the number of Polaris-type missile weapons and the continuing deployment of such ICBM weapons as the SS-11 and the SS-13, is causing grave concern in the West.

Finally, the Soviets have been mounting a vigorous public campaign on behalf of SALT in order to create a political-psychological climate in the United States which would militate against expensive new military programs whose very utility is controversial. It also serves Soviet interests to establish the impression of their peace-loving, sane, and conciliatory position before and during the negotiatory process. Thus, if such talks should become bogged down or fail, the Soviet Union could accuse the United States of bad faith and perfidy.

### Soviet Negotiatory Posture and Tactics

The Soviet Union's negotiatory profile is suggested by its declarations and tactics during the initial phases of SALT. This profile reflects several underlying objectives: the retention of a credible and stable deterrence relationship with the United States; the avoidance of a "two-front" confrontation involving China in the East and the United States and NATO in the West; and the avoidance of potentially dangerous situations deriving from tensions in the Middle East, Europe, and Asia. It is clear that as the Soviets pursue their various interests around the world, they must calculate the intensity and method of their policy pursuit so as not to compromise the above objectives. Moreover, the Soviets would seek to retain a wide range of options to deal with these policy interests, even in the event of useful strategic arms control talks with the United States.

In their negotiations, the Soviets will stress the following points:

1. Separation of strategic arms control issues from other policy issues;
2. Exclusion of matters pertaining to conventional forces;
3. Preferability of exclusive bilateral talks between the superpowers;
4. Unfettered continuation of research and development programs if production, testing, and deployment of strategic weapons are curtailed; and
5. Retention of the principle of "territorial integrity," which rejects proposals for supranational inspection.

This posture gives the Soviet Union a good bargaining position in the negotiations, since some of these points are presumably open to trade-offs with the United States.

## ALTERNATIVE SOVIET ARMS CONTROL OBJECTIVES

The Soviet Union's general approach to strategic arms limitation is that it has "no desire to receive additional unilateral advantages for itself relevant to safeguarding just its security alone."[3] Beyond this broad concept lies a multitude of possible negotiatory varia-

---

[3] "Observer," *Pravda*, March 7, 1970.

tions. The Soviets, however, refrain from going deeply into the specifics of their negotiatory position. On the U.S. side, there appears to be a similar though not identical vagueness concerning concrete and feasible negotiatory positions, though President Nixon did describe three negotiatory alternatives. First, limit the number of missiles stockpiled, which would place a ceiling on the quantity of missiles without restricting "qualitative improvements." Second, limit the number of missiles and their "capabilities, including qualitative controls over such weapons as MIRVs." Or third, reduce offensive forces without qualitative restrictions, "on the theory that at fixed and lower levels of armaments the risks of technological surprise would be reduced." Thus, the United States and, according to President Nixon, the Soviet Union, are approaching the arms limitation talks on the basis of "building blocs" for several different positions depending on "what might prove negotiable."[4]

Before the emergence of the MIRV weapons (which are being tested and are rapidly approaching the deployment stage) and the SS-9 missile (which is being deployed in sizable numbers and has undergone MRV testing), it seemed reasonable to accept the proposition that a freeze on an agreed number of launchers (which would allow for trade-offs in asymmetrical systems) would satisfy both sides and would be easily verified. The prospect of deployed MIRVs and expanded ABM systems on both sides changes this strategic equation. Thus, we have to postulate several contingent contextual situations for arms control in which to examine Soviet objectives.

[4] President Nixon, *U.S. Foreign Policy for the 1970s.*

## CRITICAL AND TOLERABLE CONDITIONS
### AFFECTING ARMS CONTROL PROSPECTS

There are a number of likely or hypothetical developments which could profoundly affect the perceptions, conduct, and outcome of arms limitation talks. These likely developments have been broken down into two broad categories—those considered "critical" and those considered "tolerable." It is assumed that critical developments could (1) imbalance severely the strategic relationship between the protagonists, thus tending to create a new "superior-inferior" relationship between them; (2) undermine the political and psychological climate necessary for negotiations; or (3) threaten a high-value objective of one or both superpowers forcing them to seek recourse in "extra" levels of deterrence capability. Tolerable developments would be likely to have a less direct and less significant impact on decisions for going ahead with strategic arms control talks, though they would still in various ways create or maintain periods of high tension. Moreover, some of these tolerable developments could rapidly become critical, depending on a variety of technological, military, political, and psychological factors.

The critical and tolerable developments listed below are not to be taken as exhaustive or equally relevant. They are merely suggestive of the kinds of problems that could affect the arms control talks.

### Critical Developments Relevant to Arms Control

1. American or Soviet deployment of a credible MIRV system;
2. American or Soviet decision to proceed with a "thick" ABM system;

3. Continued Soviet deployment of ICBMs and SLBMs (submarine launched ballistic missiles) substantially beyond present levels; and

4. Rapid development of a significant Chinese strategic nuclear capability.

Any one of the above developments would, in effect, raise doubts about the stability of deterrence and the assumed vulnerability of second-strike capabilities. It might therefore also raise the specter of surprise attacks and of a renewed search for "superiority." Deployment of a significant FOBS, MIRV, or SLBM capability by either power would negate a vital precondition for possible arms control, namely, the high credibility of verification of Soviet and American offensive and strategic levels, both quantitative and qualitative, of armament. In the event of such a deployment, it would be almost impossible to rely on extraterritorial verification methods. Moreover, even if deployment is not undertaken, but testing programs are satisfactorily concluded, both sides would be concerned lest the other clandestinely modify its "conventional" missiles into MIRVs. It would thus give impetus to those groups in the opposing country which are unwilling to accept strategic and technological "inferiority."

Other possible critical developments include:

5. Serious crises in the Middle East, East Europe, Central Europe, or Asia; and

6. Radical shifts in the Soviet or American leadership which would bring forth more militant and less reconcilable personalities into positions of power.

These developments would exacerbate the present international situation and erode the necessary preconditions for bilateral arms control negotiations. Specifically, they would result in shifts of policy priorities with a renewed stress on "vigilance," readiness, and mobilization of the nation for likely hostilities or intense political conflict.

### Tolerable Developments Relevant to Arms Control

1. American deployment of a "thin" ABM system;
2. Anticipated low-rate progression of Chinese strategic nuclear capabilities; and
3. Certain types of nuclear proliferation.

Such developments, though they might create tension and uncertainty, would not materially affect the credibility of American or Soviet deterrents or their second-strike capabilities. While such developments contain "nuisance" value, and while they may complicate the balancing of relations between the superpowers, they would not, in the final analysis, create serious obstacles or challenges to the security needs of the two countries.

4. Protracted but low-level conflicts and tensions in the Middle East and Asia; and
5. "Police actions" in superpower zones of influence.

While it is probable that these developments would not adversely affect the basic security interests of the superpowers, and therefore should not, in principle, undermine the proposed strategic arms control negotiations, much would depend on the superpowers' perceptions of the intensity and direction of such developments. In an atmosphere of high tension, poor communication, and high expectations of deterioration of the political milieu, for example, it is conceivable that events could snowball and lead to imprudent actions and commitments by the parties involved.

It may be argued that even certain "critical" conditions do not necessarily jeopardize the probability of arms control negotiations. Some argue that for negotiatory purposes it is useful to go into such talks with a "full pocket" of bargaining points which can be traded off reciprocally. Others maintain that, even in the absence of formal agreements on the limitation of strategic forces, the Soviet Union and the United States would forego plans to push on with continuous production, testing, and deployment of larger or newer strategic systems. However, such arguments are not very persuasive in the light of historical evidence. Once a weapons system has been proven to be viable and "useful," it is highly improbable that either side would agree to abandon it. The reasons for such hesitancy are many, including institutional pressures, distrust of the adversary, difficulty in verification, and much of the "mad momentum" of modern war technology.

If ideal and total solutions to the arms debacle are not possible, it is still useful to contemplate certain negotiatory arrangements which would at the very least affirm the rules of the game at potentially higher thresholds of strategic capabilities. Thus, the Soviets would likely seek such negotiatory objectives as a freeze on the number of missile launchers and thereby obtain one broad limiting parameter in the arms competition. Next, they would likely press for a moratorium on MIRV testing, after their own tests, which are behind those of the United States, have been successfully accomplished. They would also be likely to seek a moratorium on MIRV deployment with some form of verification, which by the nature of the art will be less than satisfactory. They may also seek some trade-offs in the American strategic bomber-Soviet MRBM-IRBM (medium-range and intermediate-range ballistic missiles) ratios.

At the heart of the Soviet position seems to be the belief that once political equality as well as strategic equality is obtained with the United States, a basic premise becomes established for political solutions to strategic problems. The Soviet Union, like the United States, possesses three independent types of deterrence systems, each of which could potentially inflict vast destruction on the opponent, though possibly less than what strategic parlance calls "unacceptable damage" running into tens of millions of casualties. The three systems are an offensive, land-based strategic force (SS-9, SS-11, SS-13); a growing sea-based deterrent force of SLBMs (presently inferior to that of the United States); and a significant IRBM-MRBM land-based force, which keeps West Europe, and possibly China, as "hostage." (Soviet strategic bomber forces are inferior to those of the United States.) Thus, counting on their "assured destruction" capability as sufficient to deter the United States, the Soviets are likely to consider various stabilizing arms control measures which would be less than optimal, but nevertheless tolerable.

## ALTERNATIVE OUTCOMES OF STRATEGIC ARMS LIMITATION TALKS

Realistic analysis suggests that even at their most productive point, Soviet-American arms control negotiations will not profoundly alter their adversary relationship, nor will they measurably affect the range of their traditional political interests and objectives. The negotiations would, however, stabilize and formalize Soviet-American relations and thus affirm some new rules of the game for the superpowers in the 1970s. This in itself would be a major step in the right direction which could possibly create a proper political and psychological climate for further political negotiations.

At the same time, we ought to consider some of the less desirable general implications of a potential limited arms control agreement. In any such agreement, both parties will want to retain broad options as a hedge against the eventuality that the agreement, once reached, would fail. These options would no doubt include undertaking sizable research and development programs, which would aggregate new technologies and techniques which could, in turn, generate political pressure for employing them. As long as the relations between the parties to an arms control agreement remained fairly stable, such pressures could presumably be contained. In the event, however, of a serious deterioration of relations, there would be considerable hesitation to deny self-access to available military technologies, some of which might be considered in the nature of "breakthroughs."

Let us now examine several possible outcomes of strategic arms control talks and their likely implications for superpower interests.

## Positive, Comprehensive Agreements

Optimal negotiatory arrangements in the current Soviet-American strategic arms control talks would include a freeze on land-based missile launchers at mutually acceptable current levels, a moratorium on MIRV testing (which is unlikely), a moratorium on MIRV deployment, and a limitation on future expansion of ABM systems beyond the thin level. Such an optimal arrangement would presumably fix ceilings on further deployment of SLBMs and arrive at some understanding of equitable strategic bomber and IRBM-MRBM trade-offs. Such a set of negotiatory agreements would stabilize the strategic balance at approximate parity levels, while slowing down and eventually arresting the production and deployment momentum of weapons systems on both sides.

Given the assumed Soviet negotiatory profile, it is fair to speculate that such an arms control arrangement would leave the Soviets free to pursue, rather vigorously, their hold-and-explore policy in the 1970s. It would permit them, under the umbrella of stabilized mutual deterrence, to reorder their priorities and allocations to the advantage of their nonstrategic capabilities and afford them a stronger political and military posture for the pursuit of their defensive (Chinese) and offensive (Middle East, Mediterranean, North African) policy objectives. It is doubtful, however, that the Soviets would become reckless in the use of their conventional forces for political and military exploration and expansion. Though they would have gained a stabilized strategic parity relationship with the United States, the Soviets would still expect a high U.S. resolve to use conventional forces to deter and contain any aggressive Soviet expansionistic moves, and, if necessary, to threaten to use strategic nuclear forces.

## Effects on Alliance Commitments

One of the reasons for the Soviet pressure for bilateral arms control talks at the superpower level is an implicit desire to preserve the existing superpower ascendancy in the international system. Though the idea of a superpower condominium raises concerns among the respective superpower allies, the Soviets can afford to be more sanguine about it than the United States because Soviet influence over its allies is more direct and reinforceable by threats of coercion or use of force. While Soviet and American allies would resist a bilateral superpower agreement on arms control, it would seem that the Soviets would stand to lose less in this respect than the United States. After all, it is the Soviets who sought to deny the West Germans and Japanese access to nuclear weapons in any form or shape. Moreover, much of the cohesion of the NATO alliance stems from expectations of threats from the East and the corollary reliance on the United States to protect and support West European interests which involved the Soviet Union. Hence, the possibility of a bilateral agreement for arms control could create concerns among some West European countries about the future credibility of U.S. commitments to protect their national interests.

The Soviet Union has another advantage: Soviet allies in the Warsaw Pact have expressed no interest publicly in nuclear weapons, they do not seek or expect any nuclear-sharing agreements with the Soviet Union, and they have no plans for any kind of regional nuclear-shared force. On the other hand, some West Europeans are considering a regional force as an alternative to continued and uncertain dependence on U.S. deterrence.

### Prolonged Negotiations with Partial Results

Another potential outcome of the arms control talks is one of lengthy and largely fruitless negotiations, paralleled by the constant march of military technology, resulting in some partial and essentially "tokenistic" agreements. Given the arms programs that are currently contemplated, it is fair to assume that if the talks continue much longer than one year, there will be internal pressure in both countries to implement such programs. Thus, one could assume the successful completion of MIRV tests in the United States and the Soviet Union, partial or extensive deployment of MIRV systems in both countries, expansion of current ABM programs and SLBM systems, and a general, active pursuit of their respective arms programs. Such an eventuality seems logical, since both sides would seek to strengthen their negotiatory posture as the talks continue; moreover, the action-reaction momentum would dictate resolve on either side not to fall behind the other side's arms programs.

What might be the effects of this parallel escalation of the arms race on the outcome of the talks? At the very least, it would continue to reduce the margin of negotiatory options. A progressive hardening of respective negotiatory postures might be created, while the urgency for negotiating would increase and thereby add a sense of urgency and tension to the negotiatory situation. A likely outcome might be some agreements on *what is*, i.e., making external developments legitimate by giving them the imprimatur of concessionary agreements. Such agreements might include a freeze on the number of launchers, without agreement on the "qualitative" improvements of the weapons, i.e., MIRVs. Another feasible agreement may be a new ceiling on ABM systems, with the understanding that an anti-Chinese, incremental expansion be tolerated.

Such outcomes are not to be dismissed out of hand as useless, because they would at least establish some understanding about the limitations, parameters, and tolerances of adversary initiatives. But they would on the whole be of limited utility. Essentially, they would represent forms of unilateral arms constraints under the guise of mutually agreed upon negotiatory concessions. Moreover, they would leave the strategic relations of the superpowers in a state of high tension and uncertainty and thus contribute little to a fuller stabilization of their relations.

## *Negotiations Breakdown*

Another possible outcome of the arms control talks is an early stalemate and eventual breakdown of the negotiations. This eventuality is most disturbing because it would free the action-reaction momentum to move on unrestrained, it would tend to heighten the sense of insecurity and mistrust on both sides, and it would also reinforce the arguments of those groups demanding security by superior force of arms. Having tried diplomatic means to stabilize their arms race, and having failed, both sides would most likely seek to ensure their basic interests through unilateral, available means, i.e., intensive arms programs.

The breakdown of the talks, however, would not necessarily imply a return to a war-like international milieu, nor would it necessarily mean that either or both sides would pursue irrational, unimpeded arms programs. It is very likely that some form of unilateral constraint would be imposed by economic, political, and social inhibitions, as well as by perceptions of the finiteness of arms utility beyond certain points. It may be argued that a breakdown of arms control talks, and the corollary pressures on the Soviets to "keep up" with the United States, would impose greater hardships on Moscow than on Washington. This assumption is based on the premise that the Soviets desire reasonable agreements with the United States in order to stabilize their western flank and free themselves to pursue other policy opportunities elsewhere. A breakdown in such talks would jeopardize these assumed objectives and would force the Soviets to spread their resources and attention quite widely, thus stretching their capabilities rather severely.

Unilateral constraint in a highly unpredictable situation with a high probability of strategic-technological surprise is not a very sound basis for defense policy decisions. It could be fairly assumed, therefore, that sooner or later such constraint would give way to doubts and pressures and would result in a search for higher levels of security. Such a search would encompass parts or all of the presently available and possible panoply of weapons systems. A "thick" ABM, an extensive MIRV deployment, or an improved FOBS would tend to destabilize the deterrence relationship and would create added tensions in international relations. Threshold powers might then resign themselves to the abandonment of nuclear options, or, alternatively, they might exercise such options through independent or regional nuclear forces. If such a deployment of new strategic systems created high levels of tension and uncertainties about credible deterrence, it might also lead to unilateral revocation of earlier arms control agreements such as the Test Ban and Nonproliferation Treaties.

## CONCLUSION

The Soviet Union's arms control interests are shaped, on the one hand, by concerns about its basic and current security needs and, on the other hand, by its short-range and long-range policy objectives. The former motivates Soviet leaders to seek formal stabilization of Soviet-American strategic relations from a position of equality; the latter motivates them to seek a wide range of flexible options for the pursuit of their broad policy interests—including contingencies in the event the arms control talks fail, and even if they yield agreements.

On balance, it seems reasonable to suggest that relative equality in American and Soviet strategic capabilities is a useful basis for arms control negotiations, and in a broader sense, a reasonable basis for the pursuit of U.S. security interests. As indicated earlier, policies in pursuit of strategic superiority have in the past resulted in expensive and politically detrimental destabilizations of international relations; they have created action-reaction trends which resulted in accelerated arms programs; they have brought about situations in which an initial arms advantage on one side is nullified by progress on the other; and they have also resulted in over-reactions by one or the other protagonist which only propelled the arms race further. Large and growing strategic weapons systems have limited applicability to problems and issues that involve nonnuclear countries, since the latter are undeterred by such capabilities in pursuing their national objectives. Consequently, a freeze of strategic offensive and defensive weapons at current or future force levels seems useful to U.S. interests. For such an agreement to be realistic and viable, however, it should be coupled with a formal or informal Soviet-American understanding on several issues:

*Regulation of Research and Development Levels and the Testing of New Weapons Systems.* Verification and control of research and development programs is a highly difficult and complex problem that has strong political overtones. It is unlikely that either partner in the talks would desire to curtail such programs sharply, since they provide necessary options and fallback positions in the event of an abrogation of agreements. Procedures for examining budgetary allocations may offer a minimal control device for the verification of research and development levels. The testing of new weapons systems is, in principle, more verifiable. Some kind of agreement would be necessary to ensure that weapons tests did not involve weapons prohibited by any arms control agreements.

*Termination of Currently Ongoing Programs for the Deployment of Offensive and Defensive Weapons Systems.* The Soviet Union is presently involved in active production and deployment programs of weapons systems, including SLBMs and ICBMs. Both the Soviet

Union and the United States have been testing MIRVs and/or FOBSs. It is important that these programs are taken into account in the early stages of the talks, lest they make such arms control talks academic.

*Countermeasures Regarding Third Parties Who May Seriously Threaten an Agreed Upon Strategic Stabilization.* The problem of how to go about assuring a superpower strategic stabilization which may be threatened by an aggressive or irresponsible third nuclear power is complicated by a host of domestic, political, and military problems. While such an arrangement is not absolutely necessary for successful arms control talks, it may be useful to consider the matter in connection with the other issues relevant to arms control.

*Augmentation of Conventional Forces, Either Independently or in Regional Defense Alliances.* It is assumed here that in the event of a strategic arms freeze the Soviet Union would be motivated to strengthen and upgrade its conventional forces and would likely employ them more actively for defense and policy purposes. The West must retain wide options for dealing with such likely contingencies as they emerge.

It would be imprudent of the United States to base its security interests and policies on expectations of Soviet technological and economic backwardness. The Soviet Union has in the past shown an impressive ability to make great strides in catching up with, matching, and at times surpassing western progress in the development and deployment of strategic forces. It would be equally imprudent to assume that the current Soviet leadership is planning to commit its economic and social systems to vast arming programs with the intent to go to nuclear war. The constraints of the deterrence relationship and current domestic issues seem to argue against such an assumption. A strategic arms control agreement would enhance relations between the superpowers and, at the same time, would serve their individual needs.

# Appendix

## A. Soviet Military Capabilities, 1950–1968

| Year | Budget (*billion rubles*) | Armed Forces (*millions*) | ICBMs | MRBMs and IRBMs | Submarines, Conventional | Submarines, Nuclear |
|------|------|------|------|------|------|------|
| 1950 | 82.9 | 2.8 | | | 360 | |
| 1951 | 96.4 | 4.6 | | | 370 | |
| 1952 | 108.6 | | | | 370 | |
| 1953 | 110.2 | | | | | |
| 1954 | 100.3[a] | 4.75 | | | 370 | |
| 1955 | 112.1[b] | 5.76[c] | | | 400 | |
| 1956 | 102.5 | | | | | |
| 1957 | 96.7 | 3.8–4.2[c] | | | 500 | |
| 1958 | 93.6 | | | | 500 | |
| 1959 | 96.1 | 3.9 | | | | |
| 1960 | 93.6 | | 1–10 | | 450 | |
| 1961 | 11.9 | 3.8 | 50 | 200 | 450 | |
| 1962 | 13.4 | 3.6 | 75 | 700 | 410 | 10 |
| 1963 | 13.9 | 3.3 | 100 | 750 | 420 | 20 |
| 1964 | 13.3 | 3.3 | 200 | 700–750 | 400 | 30 |
| 1965 | 12.8[d] | 3.15 | 425 | 700–750 | 370 | 40 |
| 1966 | 13.4 | 3.165 | 400–450 | 700–750 | 350 | 50 |
| 1967 | 14.5 | 3.22 | 720 | 750 | 330 | 50 |
| 1968 | 16.0 | 3.1–3.3 | 900 | 700–900 | 350–400 | 40–50 |
| 1969 | 17.7 | 3.3 | 1,100 | 700 | 320 | 60 |

[a] The Malenkov defense budget for 1953–54 went from 110 billion rubles to 100 billion rubles, although Soviet force levels remained fairly stable.

[b] The 1954–55 defense budget forced through by Malenkov's opponents went from 100.3 to 112.1 billion rubles. Force levels were also increased.

[c] Between 1955–57 the Soviet government reduced the standing forces by about 40 per cent and yet the defense budget remained relatively high at 102 billion rubles.

[d] Khrushchev's last budget was to decrease the defense allocations from 13.3 billion new rubles (one new ruble equals ten old ones) to 12.8, despite strong internal pressures for a substantial increase of the defense budget. After his ouster the new regime reinstated old budgetary levels which have been increasing yearly ever since.

*Note:* Official Soviet defense budgetary figures do not reveal the actual amounts allocated, which are believed to be about triple the announced figures. They do, however, indicate the actual size of the defense budgets relative to previous years and to the total national budgets.

*Source:* Adapted from *Military Balance* (London: Institute for Strategic Studies), *Jane's Fighting Ships* (New York: McGraw-Hill) and the *Statesman's Year Book* (New York: St. Martin's Press).

**B. U.S. Defense Budget, Federal Budget, and GNP for Selected Years**

(billion dollars)

| Fiscal Years | GNP | Federal Budget Outlays | | | | Dept. of Defense Outlays as Percent of: | |
|---|---|---|---|---|---|---|---|
| | | Net total | Dept. of Defense | Other | Offsets[a] | GNP | Federal budget |
| 1950 (lowest year since World War II)[b] | $ 263.3 | $ 43.1 | $11.9 | $ 31.2 | na | 4.5 | 27.7 |
| 1953 (Korea peak)[b] | 358.9 | 76.8 | 47.7 | 29.1 | na | 13.3 | 62.1 |
| 1961 | 506.5 | 97.8 | 44.6 | 55.7 | −2.5 | 8.8 | 44.5 |
| 1964 (last prewar year) | 612.2 | 118.6 | 50.8 | 70.7 | −2.9 | 8.3 | 41.8 |
| 1968 (SEA peak)[b] | 822.6 | 178.9 | 78.0 | 105.5 | −4.6 | 9.5 | 42.5 |
| 1969 | 900.6 | 184.6 | 78.7 | 111.0 | −5.1 | 8.7 | 41.5 |
| 1970 (Johnson budget) | 960.0 | 195.3 | 81.6[c] | 119.4 | −5.7 | 8.5 | 40.6 |
| 1970 (current estimate) | 960.0 | 197.9 | 77.0 | 127.0 | −6.1 | 8.0 | 37.7 |
| 1971 (budget estimate)[d] | 1,020.0 | 200.8 | 71.8 | 135.6 | −6.6 | 7.0 | 34.6 |
| 1971 (in 1964 dollars) | | | 54.6 | | | | |
| Changes 1964 to 1971 | +407.8 | +82.2 | +21.0[e] | +64.9 | −3.7 | | |
| 1969 to 1971 | +119.4 | +16.2 | −6.9 | +24.6 | −1.5 | | |

[a] These amounts are undistributed intragovernmental transactions deducted from government-wide totals. These include government contributions for employee retirement and interest received by trust funds.

[b] Measured in terms of Defense outlays as a percentage of GNP and federal budget.

[c] Includes the $2.6 billion cost of the July 1, 1969 pay raise. The pay-raise costs were not shown in the agency totals, but were included in a government-wide contingency estimate in the fiscal year 1970 Johnson budget.

[d] Lowest percent of GNP since 1951; lowest percent of the federal budget since 1950.

[e] This is 5.2 percent of the GNP growth during this period, and 24.4 percent of the increase in the federal budget.

## C. Equivalent Megatonnage of U.S. 1967 Strategic Missiles

| Missile Type | Number of Missiles (N) | | Yield (Y) | Equivalent Megatons ($N \times Y^{2/3}$) | |
|---|---|---|---|---|---|
| | Case 1[a] | Case 2[b] | | Case 1[a] | Case 2[b] |
| Minuteman I | 500 | 0 | 1+ | 500 | 0 |
| Minuteman II | 500 | 1,000 | 2 | 790 | 1,580 |
| Polaris A1, A2, A3 | 656 | 656 | 0.7 | 520 | 520 |
| Titan II | 54 | 54 | 5+ | 160 | 160 |
| Total stockpiled megaton equivalents | | | | 1,970 | 2,260 |

[a] Presumes Minuteman stockpile divided between models I and II.
[b] Presumes Minuteman stockpile is all model II.
*Source:* Daniel J. Fink, "Strategic Warfare," *Science and Technology,* October 1968.

# Index

Adenauer, Konrad, 158
Africa, 56, 93, 142, 143, 184, 194
Air Defense Forces (PVO), 13–14, 27
Albania, 145n, 152
Antiballistic missile (ABM), 60, 62, 131, 131n, 176, 198; Kosygin on, 19; Moscow system, 4; Soviet scientific opinion on, 11; and SALT, 3, 66, 187–88, 190, 194, 196, 197; U.S. program, 4, 5, 184; Lt. Gen. Zavialov on, 15n
Arab countries, 102, 104; Israeli war (1967), 152
Arms control, 178–79, 181; prospects for negotiations, 60, 60n, 67, 68, 191. See also China, Communist, on arms control
Arms control, Soviet Union, 55, 56; and defensive missile systems, 4, 60; and economic considerations, 5–7; effect of China on, 131, 145, 146; effect on allies of, 8; effect on SALT of, 196; incentives for, 20, 57, 136; interest groups involved in, 9–12; military establishment position on, 12–14; and nonnuclear countries, 54, 145; and Nonproliferation Treaty, 66; and nuclear proliferation, 74; and role in Soviet policy, 40, 42; and Soviet policy toward China, 123; and Soviet scientists, 10; and West Germany, 150. See also Arms freeze
Arms control agreement, 4, 7, 24, 49, 66, 193, 202
Arms freeze, 180, 191, 200, 201; Soviet Union and United States, 59, 194, 197
Arms race, 43, 62, 66, 101, 200; Krushchev on, 30; military considerations on, 3
Asia, 90, 94, 142, 143, 185, 189
Austria, 167

Balance of power: China and, 139; Soviet Union, nonproliferation as prerequisite for stability, 79; strategic balance, 29, 31, 198
Belovskii, D., 53
Bipolarity. See Strategic relationship, Soviet-American
Brest-Litovsk, treaty of, 168
Brezhnev, Leonid, 32, 45, 129n, 142, 150, 176; on defense, 44; on military resource allocation, 6
Bulgaria, 163, 169
Bundeswehr, 95, 158
Bundy, McGeorge, 57, 58, 63, 182